IoT Projects with Bluetooth Low Energy

Harness the power of connected things

Madhur Bhargava

BIRMINGHAM - MUMBAI

IoT Projects with Bluetooth Low Energy

First published: August 2017

Production reference: 1280817

Published by Packt Publishing Ltd.
Livery Place
35 Livery Street
Birmingham
B3 2PB, UK.

ISBN 978-1-78839-944-9

www.packtpub.com

Credits

Author
Madhur Bhargava

Reviewers
Jacqueline Wilson
Gustavo Litovsky

Commissioning Editor
Gebin George

Acquisition Editor
Divya Poojari

Content Development Editor
Dattatraya More

Technical Editor
Sneha Hanchate

Copy Editor
Laxmi Subramanian

Project Coordinator
Shweta H Birwatkar

Proofreader
Safis Editing

Indexer
Mariammal Chettiyar

Graphics
Tania Dutta

Production Coordinator
Shantanu Zagade

Foreword

This book is fun, disguised as education.

Many folks say that the best way to learn something is by doing it. Even more effective, though, is building something tangible that can immediately be put to use. With this in mind, the book you have in your hands is an impressive accomplishment!

Let's not fool ourselves. Nobody will be able to survive in a technical field without the drive and ability to learn new things. Staying current in this industry can be quite challenging. Aside from the rapid pace with which technology evolves, there's often a palpable tedium of trudging through dry technical materials. One's mind can wander easily. Paragraphs have to be reread several times. Interruptions can feel like blessings.

This book is not like that.

Its title, IoT Projects with Bluetooth Low Energy, is a bit humble. To start off with the book, Madhur Bhargava breaks down the intricacies of the BLE protocol using a conversational voice. Almost without realizing it, the reader internalizes highly technical information, progressing to a full understanding of BLE. To read only that first chapter would be worth the investment of time and money into this book. But there's more! Madhur then accomplishes a feat rare among technical authors. Using the same delivery technique, he provides instructions on building a series of full-stack apps and covering several diverse technologies, without alienating the audience.

Fellow reader, the book's title might *suggest* that you will learn BLE -- and you will -- but you will learn so much more. *Without even intending to.*

Somehow, by chapter 4, I had coded multiple versions of mobile apps on both major platforms. I am not a mobile programmer; nor did I rely on copying and pasting code from the companion Github repo. Still, from Madhur's careful explanations, I understood every line of code used in the projects. The short, sweet introductions to Firebase, Xcode, Android Studio and emulators were enough to get me productive in each of them. While I do have programming experience, I haven't created much in Swift or Java. I have to credit the author with being thorough and keeping the instructions straightforward and focused. You will finish this book wanting to learn and do more. There are not enough books like this.

Finally, I should issue a warning. This book may start a costly addiction. If you don't already have the hardware for these projects, you will want it. I have Raspberry Pis, sensors, beacons, Android devices... all sitting in front of me as I write this.

Enjoy your adventure! Time for me to go play with my new toys now.

Jacqueline Wilson

Assistant Professor of Computer Science

Cecil College

About the Author

Madhur Bhargava holds a bachelor's degree in electronics and communication, after which he did a specialization in Wireless and Mobile Computing at CDAC ACTS Pune, India. He started his career at Electronic Arts as a trainee software engineer working on mobile games and eventually moved on to address problems in personalized healthcare, leveraging the power of mobile computing.

He is proficient in various mobile/embedded technologies and strives to be a software generalist. Since the inception of his career, he has worked extensively with various mobile technologies, such as Android, iOS, J2ME, Brew, Blackberry OS, and Xamarin. He has designed and developed Bluetooth Low Energy applications pertaining to the healthcare and automation domains for both Android and iOS platforms.

He believes that good software is the result of talented individuals working together as a communicative team in an Agile manner. He is both a Certified Scrum Master and a Certified Xamarin Developer.

Apart from work, he likes to spend time with family, read, and watch movies.

Dedicated to my family and to the team of amazing people I am working with. They are the reason that made this book happen.

About the Reviewer

Jacqueline Wilson has degrees in computer science and information management systems. She has an affinity for cutting edge technology, shiny gadgets, and technical books. Several years ago, she discovered the perfect way to channel her passion, and currently works as an assistant professor of computer science at Cecil College in North East, MD, where her aim is to make learning fun again. She lives in an old farmhouse filled with techie projects, along with her very accommodating husband, son, two dogs, four cats, and two fish.

Gustavo Litovsky is a lifelong engineer and expert on Bluetooth, Wi-Fi, and other wireless communications. As the founder and CEO of Argenox Technologies, he leads a team of engineers building amazing connected products for some of the world's most recognizable brands, as well as numerous startups. Prior to founding Argenox, he spent time consulting at Samsung and several other companies on integrating wireless connectivity. He previously worked as an engineer at Texas Instrument's Wireless Connectivity business unit, supporting customers with Wi-Fi, Bluetooth, and GPS solutions for products such as the Nike FuelBand, Pebble Smartwatch, and Motorola Droid Bionic. He is also an inventor and co-inventor of several patents.

I would like to thank my wife, Rebecca, without whose help and support nothing would get done. To my parents and children, for all their love and support.

www.PacktPub.com

For support files and downloads related to your book, please visit www.PacktPub.com.

Did you know that Packt offers eBook versions of every book published, with PDF and ePub files available? You can upgrade to the eBook version at www.PacktPub.com and as a print book customer, you are entitled to a discount on the eBook copy. Get in touch with us at service@packtpub.com for more details.

At www.PacktPub.com, you can also read a collection of free technical articles, sign up for a range of free newsletters and receive exclusive discounts and offers on Packt books and eBooks.

https://www.packtpub.com/mapt

Get the most in-demand software skills with Mapt. Mapt gives you full access to all Packt books and video courses, as well as industry-leading tools to help you plan your personal development and advance your career.

Why subscribe?

- Fully searchable across every book published by Packt
- Copy and paste, print, and bookmark content
- On demand and accessible via a web browser

Customer Feedback

Thanks for purchasing this Packt book. At Packt, quality is at the heart of our editorial process. To help us improve, please leave us an honest review on this book's Amazon page at https://www.amazon.com/dp/1788399447.

If you'd like to join our team of regular reviewers, you can e-mail us at customerreviews@packtpub.com. We award our regular reviewers with free eBooks and videos in exchange for their valuable feedback. Help us be relentless in improving our products!

Table of Contents

Preface

Bluetooth Low Energy is one of the key cornerstones of the IoT paradigm. This book intends to bridge the gap between the theoretical and practical understanding of Bluetooth Low Energy by first introducing the reader to Bluetooth Low Energy and then creating a practical understanding of the subject on top of that theoretical foundation by building four hands-on Bluetooth Low Energy projects focused on IoT.

You will be leveraging existing popular mobile technologies (Android and iOS) to design IoT-oriented applications that will interact with various Bluetooth Low Energy based hardware and sensors such as Raspberry Pi, iTags, Fitness Trackers, and TI SensorTag.

What this book covers

Chapter 1, *What is Bluetooth Low Energy*, introduces the reader to Bluetooth Low Energy and its various building blocks—Profiles, Services, Characteristics, and Descriptors.

Chapter 2, *Setting Up*, sets up the development environment to execute the Android and iOS code samples included in the book.

Chapter 3, *Building a Service Explorer App*, solidifies our understanding of the concepts introduced in the first chapter by building a Service Explorer app that can be used to explore services on any Bluetooth Low Energy device. We eventually use the same app to explore services on a fitness tracker, read heart rate data, and upload it to a remote Firebase backend.

Chapter 4, *Designing a Personal Tracking System*, focuses on a key concept in IoT, that is, proximity. We design a Personal Tracker app using an iTag. The app uses the RSSI received from an iTag to approximate the distance between the app-hosting device and the iTag.

Chapter 5, *Beacons with Raspberry Pi*, introduces the reader to one of the key cornerstones of IoT, that is, Beacons, and the two primary Beacon protocols—Eddystone and iBeacon. In addition, we also configure a Raspberry Pi to be used as an Eddystone Beacon and write an Android and iOS app to detect it.

Chapter 6, *Weather Monitoring Using BLE in Warehouses*, shows you how to combine the knowledge that you gained in the previous chapters and address a real-life problem revolving around BLE and IoT. We introduce a new sensor type and build a Weather Monitoring app using that sensor.

Chapter 7, *Going Further*, discusses the future of BLE and IoT by introducing the reader to various use cases and products based on Bluetooth Low Energy, that are already available or will become available on the consumer market in the future.

What you need for this book

This book will guide you through the installation of all the tools that you need to follow the code samples. Code samples introduced in various chapters are for both Android and iOS platforms hence you will need to install the Android Studio and XCode IDEs. Since simulators lack Bluetooth functionality, hence you will need physical Android and iOS devices to run the code samples. In terms of hardware, you will be needing a Raspberry Pi for the Code Lab specific for Chapter 5, *Beacons with Raspberry Pi*. For Chapter 4, *Designing a Personal Tracking System*, and Chapter 6, *Weather Monitoring Using BLE in Warehouses*, you will be needing a very low cost iTag and the Texas Instruments Sensor Tag. All of the hardware can be easily procured online.

Who this book is for

This book is intended for anyone with a technical bend of mind who wants to gain practical knowledge of BLE via its usage in IoT projects. Although the book has a fairly practical undertone, it starts by building a theoretical foundation of Bluetooth Low Energy, finally using that foundation as a platform to design practical projects and solutions, and hence it can be picked up by novices and experts alike.

Conventions

In this book, you will find a number of styles of text that distinguish between different kinds of information. Here are some examples of these styles, and an explanation of their meaning.

Code words in text, folder names, filenames, and file extensions are shown as follows:

"Double-click on the downloaded .dmg file and in the shown dialog, copy the Android Studio executable to the Applications directory."

A block of code is set as follows:

```
private void initialiseBluetooth() {
bluetoothManager =
(BluetoothManager)getSystemService
(Context.BLUETOOTH_SERVICE);
bluetoothAdapter = bluetoothManager.getAdapter();
bluetoothLeScanner = bluetoothAdapter.getBluetoothLeScanner();
}
```

When we wish to draw your attention to a particular part of a code block, the relevant lines or items are set in bold:

```
bluetoothAdapter = bluetoothManager.getAdapter();
bluetoothLeScanner = bluetoothAdapter.getBluetoothLeScanner();
```

Any command-line, (including commands at the R console) input or output is written as follows:

```
$ npm install --save eddystone-beacon
```

New terms and **important words** are shown in bold. Words that you see on the screen, in menus or dialog boxes for example, appear in the text like this: "Clicking the **Next** button moves you to the next screen."

Warnings or important notes appear in a box like this.

Tips and tricks appear like this.

Reader feedback

Feedback from our readers is always welcome. Let us know what you think about this book-what you liked or disliked. Reader feedback is important for us as it helps us develop titles that you will really get the most out of. To send us general feedback, simply e-mail feedback@packtpub.com, and mention the book's title in the subject of your message. If there is a topic that you have expertise in and you are interested in either writing or contributing to a book, see our author guide at www.packtpub.com/authors.

Customer support

Now that you are the proud owner of a Packt book, we have a number of things to help you to get the most from your purchase.

Downloading the example code

You can download the example code files for this book from your account at http://www.packtpub.com. If you purchased this book elsewhere, you can visit http://www.packtpub.com/support and register to have the files e-mailed directly to you.

You can download the code files by following these steps:

1. Log in or register to our website using your e-mail address and password.
2. Hover the mouse pointer on the **SUPPORT** tab at the top.
3. Click on **Code Downloads & Errata**.
4. Enter the name of the book in the **Search** box.
5. Select the book for which you're looking to download the code files.
6. Choose from the drop-down menu where you purchased this book from.
7. Click on **Code Download**.

Once the file is downloaded, please make sure that you unzip or extract the folder using the latest version of:

* WinRAR / 7-Zip for Windows
* Zipeg / iZip / UnRarX for Mac
* 7-Zip / PeaZip for Linux

The code bundle for the book is also hosted on GitHub at
`https://github.com/PacktPublishing/IoT-Projects-with-Bluetooth-Low-Energy`. We
also have other code bundles from our rich catalog of books and videos available at
`https://github.com/PacktPublishing/`. Check them out!

Downloading the color images of this book

We also provide you with a PDF file that has color images of the screenshots/diagrams used
in this book. The color images will help you better understand the changes in the output.
You can download this file from
`https://www.packtpub.com/sites/default/files/downloads/IoTProjectswithBluetooth`
`LowEnergy_ColorImages.pdf`.

Errata

Although we have taken every care to ensure the accuracy of our content, mistakes do
happen. If you find a mistake in one of our books-maybe a mistake in the text or the code-
we would be grateful if you could report this to us. By doing so, you can save other readers
from frustration and help us improve subsequent versions of this book. If you find any
errata, please report them by visiting `http://www.packtpub.com/submit-errata`, selecting
your book, clicking on the **Errata Submission Form** link, and entering the details of your
errata. Once your errata are verified, your submission will be accepted and the errata will
be uploaded to our website or added to any list of existing errata under the Errata section of
that title.

To view the previously submitted errata, go to
`https://www.packtpub.com/books/content/support` and enter the name of the book in the
search field. The required information will appear under the **Errata** section.

Piracy

Piracy of copyrighted material on the Internet is an ongoing problem across all media. At
Packt, we take the protection of our copyright and licenses very seriously. If you come
across any illegal copies of our works in any form on the Internet, please provide us with
the location address or website name immediately so that we can pursue a remedy.

Please contact us at `copyright@packtpub.com` with a link to the suspected pirated
material.

We appreciate your help in protecting our authors and our ability to bring you valuable content.

Questions

If you have a problem with any aspect of this book, you can contact us at `questions@packtpub.com`, and we will do our best to address the problem.

1
What is Bluetooth Low Energy?

The internet of things will augment your brain.

– Eric Schmidt

At a very basic level IoT can be described as a network of things (physical devices, vehicles, buildings, and what not), which when augmented with sensors and servers enables these objects or things to collect and exchange data. A major driver behind this growth has been the advent of a comparatively lesser-known technology known as **Bluetooth Low Energy (BLE)**.

In this chapter, we discuss this technology in the light of the following topics:

- An Overview of Bluetooth Low Energy
- The Need for Bluetooth Low Energy
- Bluetooth Low Energy versus Bluetooth Classic
- Architecture of Bluetooth Low Energy
- Profiles
- Services
- Characteristics
- Indications
- Notifications
- Bluetooth 5, Meshes, and Beacons

An Overview of Bluetooth Low Energy

Bluetooth Low Energy or Bluetooth Smart is a comparatively new wireless communication technology that was introduced by the Bluetooth Special Interest Group in 2010. Although the technology itself was being developed way earlier by Nokia around 2001 to 2006 under the name Wibree, it was not until 2007 that an agreement was reached with the various members of Bluetooth SIG that Wibree should now be included in the Core Bluetooth Specification, a task which was completed in 2010, when Wibree became a part of Bluetooth Core Specification version 4.0 as Bluetooth Smart, commonly known as Bluetooth Low Energy (its original name). The first mobile device to incorporate the 4.0 specification was iPhone 4S. However, as it is almost always with early adopters, the then iPhone 4S operating system did have some bugs regarding Bluetooth connectivity and range sometimes being poor. Bluetooth Smart technology has matured rapidly since then and come a long way. In fact, the dawn of the current IoT revolution is relying significantly on Bluetooth Low Energy for its success. According to an analysis done by IndustryArc.

 To read the detailed report from IndustryArc, please visit: `http://industryarc.com/PressRelease/43/bluetooth-smart-lowenergy.html`.

Bluetooth Low Energy device shipments are forecast to increase to 8.4 billion units by 2020 at a mean annual growth rate of 29% which eventually will also lead to a surge in the number of IoT devices (things, if spoken semantically). We are seeing the early stages of this revolution all around us as a result of which, almost every handheld device and wearable nowadays has BLE capabilities.

So, what is it that makes Bluetooth Low Energy so special? How is Bluetooth Low Energy different from the good old regular Bluetooth? Why is every other wearable device (for example, Fitbit, Nike Fuelband, Apple watch and maybe your own smartphone) on the market using Bluetooth Low Energy (*Couldn't they just do away with regular bluetooth and be happy about it*)? We will explore the answer to all these questions and many others in this chapter. Furthermore, we will also discuss the architecture and what lies under the hood that makes Bluetooth Low Energy live up to its name.

To know more about bluetooth visit `https://www.bluetooth.com/` and for a PDF sample, go to `http://www.industryarc.com/pdfdownload.php?id=187`

The Need for Bluetooth Low Energy

So, coming to the very first question, what makes Bluetooth Low Energy so special? We will have to go back in time a little bit to address this.

During the year 2001, the researchers at Nokia had already identified a number of scenarios, which were not being addressed by any of the existing **Wireless Personal Area Network** (**WPAN**) communication technologies,

WPAN or a Wireless Personal Area Network is a network centered around a user's personal space. The typical range for a WPAN network is around 10 meters. An example of a WPAN network technology is Bluetooth.

The most common factors that came out as a result of studying these scenarios were:

- Low power usage
- Low cost
- Minimal differences with current Bluetooth technology

Hence, what started in 2001 ended up being Bluetooth Low Energy or Bluetooth Smart in 2010. The technology was given a descriptive name, which also describes its real purpose of existence. Bluetooth Low Energy was designed for devices which had:

- Low power requirements, operating on a coin cell for longer periods of time (months or even years)
- Low cost
- Industry standard wireless protocol, which can be easily adopted

And guess what? They finally succeeded in achieving all the set goals.
If you remember the age of early mobile phones, the ones which had classic Bluetooth only, then you might remember that classic Bluetooth was a battery-expensive feature and continuous usage used to drain the battery on the device pretty quickly. Also, there were not many low-cost Bluetooth accessories available as there are now. However, with the advent of Bluetooth Low Energy (which consumes low power), all these things are bygones. We can now buy a Bluetooth tag, which supports and operates on Bluetooth 4.0, similar to the ones shown next for as low as 1-2 euros (Don't worry too much if you do not yet understand what this tag is used for. In the later chapters, we will build an application around the usage of this tag.):

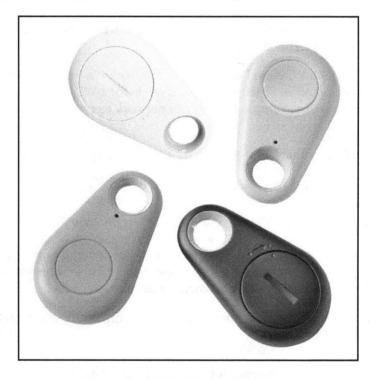

Figure 1: Low Cost Bluetooth Smart Tag

Fitbit, one of the most common and popular fitness trackers, used for recording the body vitals and daily activity, has a battery life of 7-10 days after a full charge (source: `https://www.fitbit.com/charge`). Please note that this is a device which is working continuously day and night and even records data when you are sleeping:

Figure 2. Fitbits; source: `dev.fitbit.com`

Lastly, Bluetooth Low Energy is now being incorporated in each and every smartphone being rolled out. Apple which was one of the early adopters of Bluetooth Low Energy was later joined by Samsung, LG, Motorola, and every other major mobile device manufacturer out there. The popularity and adoption rate of the technology has already seen exponential growth and with the announcement of Bluetooth 5, which promises double the speed and four times the range, we will continue to see an even larger wave of Bluetooth Low Energy and IoT devices hitting the market.

Bluetooth Low Energy versus Bluetooth Classic

Although Bluetooth Classic and Bluetooth Low Energy share many important things such as architecture, and both operate in 2.4 GHz ISM Band, the fundamental difference between them is that BLE is designed to consume less power. Due to this caveat, BLE is not an ideal candidate for applications such as streaming voice data (talking over the phone); however it makes BLE an excellent choice when it comes to communicating via exchanging small amounts of data over short periods of time. We shall discuss the communication differences between Bluetooth Classic and Bluetooth Low Energy in detail below.

Under Bluetooth Classic, when two or more devices want to talk to each other, then they always need to pair first (although pairing does happen when two devices communicate over Bluetooth Low Energy too, however; it is not mandatory in the case of BLE). Once the pairing has succeeded, an ad hoc network is established also known as the **piconet**:

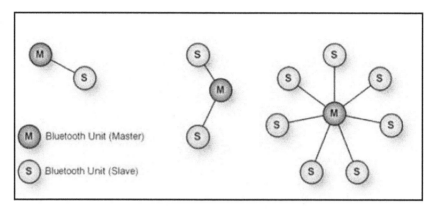

Figure 3: A master-slave piconet; source: https://goo.gl/O9tgEB

A piconet can consist of a single master and up to seven slave devices. The devices can switch role by agreement (a slave can become a master at a later stage during the timeline of communication). Although a master can have up to seven slaves, at any point in time the master is addressing a single slave and the slave is supposed to listen when this happens. Also, it is important to note that being a slave to more than one master is certainly possible. This often results in interconnected piconets, also known as a **scatternet**:

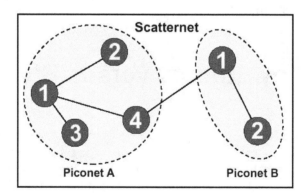

Figure 4: A scatternet; source: https://goo.gl/WXixBp

Whether it is piconet or scatternet, the communication channel between the master and slave remains established even if no data is being exchanged and is only terminated when one (or both) of the parties (master/slave) explicitly decides to terminate the connection.

On the other hand, communication over Bluetooth Low Energy can be abstracted away as *interacting with a really intelligent database*. During this type of communication, each of the devices involved either plays the role of the database (known as peripheral in Bluetooth Low Energy terminology) or a listener (known as central in Bluetooth Low Energy terminology) of that database updates. Whenever new data is available, the database *magically* notifies all its listeners that new data is available to use. This magic takes place via something known as *Indications* and *Notifications* which we shall elaborate on in an upcoming section:

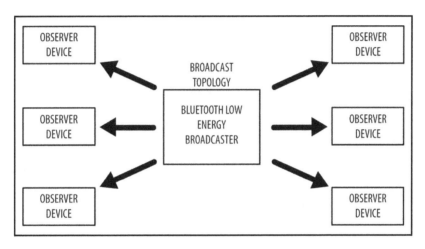

Figure 5: Bluetooth Low Energy communication; source: learn.adafruit.com

Before moving on to rest of the differences between Bluetooth Low Energy and Bluetooth Classic (also known as Bluetooth BR/EDR), let's first discuss a few terms, the understanding of which is absolutely critical for the discussion ahead:

- **ISM channels/radio bands**: ISM bands are the portions of the electromagnetic frequency spectrum, which are reserved for industrial, scientific, and medical purposes only. For example, the 2.4GHz ISM band is available worldwide and spans 2400MHz to 2483.5MHz. This means a device operating in this band can be legally used anywhere in the world (provided it is certified).
- **Data rate**: This is the *theoretical* rate of data flow, which can be achieved in a system.
- **Application throughput**: This is the *practical* rate of data flow, which can be achieved in a system.

Both Bluetooth Classic (BR/EDR) and Bluetooth Low Energy operate in the 2400-2483.5 MHz range within the ISM 2.4 GHz frequency band. However, data exchange in Bluetooth Classic happens over one of the 79 designated channels, as opposed to that of Bluetooth Low Energy where the number of designated channels is 40:

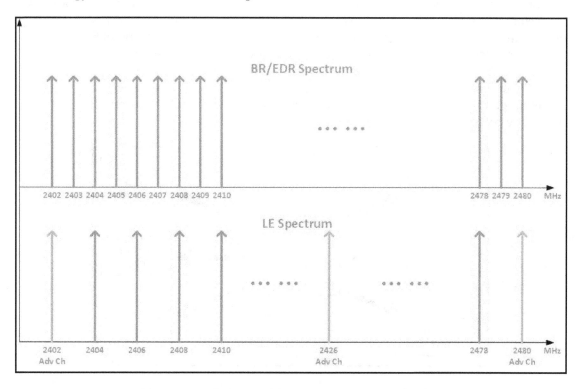

Figure 6: RF spectrum for Bluetooth and BLE

The core technical specifications of Bluetooth Classic and Bluetooth Low Energy are tabulated as follows:

Technical specifications	Bluetooth Low Energy	Bluetooth Classic
Power consumption	Rated power Consumption of 0.01 to 0.5 W	Rated power consumption of 1 W
Data rate and throughput	Physical data rate is 1 MBit/s with an effective application data throughput of 0.3 MBit/s	Physical data rate is 1-3 MBit/s with an effective application data throughput of 2.1 MBit/s

Latency (from a non-connected state)	6 ms	100 ms
Voice capable	No	Yes
Distance/range (theoretical max.)	>100 m	100 m
Pairing mandatory	No	Yes
Frequency (GHz)	2.4	2.4
Active slaves	Up to 7	Undefined and implementation dependent
Security	128-bit AES and application layer user defined	56/128-bit and application layer user defined
Network topology	Point-to-point and Star	Piconet, scatternet, and point-to-point
Frequency channels	40	79
Minimum total time to send data (det. battery life)	3 ms	100 ms
Current consumption	<15 mA	<30 mA
Logo	Bluetooth SMART	Bluetooth®

Architecture of Bluetooth Low Energy

The architecture of Bluetooth Low Energy is divided into three important layers:

- **Application**
- **Host**
- **Controller**

Refer to the following figure:

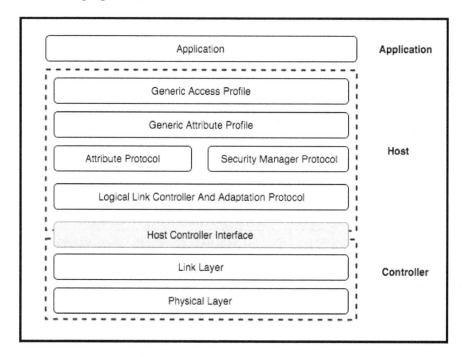

Figure 9: Bluetooth Low Energy architecture

We shall touch on every segment/layer briefly before delving deeper into each of the layers.

Application

We will develop multiple applications for several IoT and Bluetooth Low Energy use cases throughout the course of this book and these applications will be hosted in the application layer of a Bluetooth Low Energy compatible device. This is the layer which will contain the user interface, application logic, and the overall application architecture.

A working knowledge of this layer is necessary to start building Bluetooth Low Energy oriented applications. However, it is always good to know what goes under the hood and how our application talks to the underlying Bluetooth Low Energy hardware/chipset; hence, we will also explore the host and the controller layers.

Host

Lying just the following **Application** layer is the **Host** layer, which has the following layers:

- **Generic Access Profile** (**GAP**): This defines how Bluetooth Low Energy devices access and communicate with each other. Bluetooth Low Energy devices can connect to each other in one of the following roles:
    - **Broadcaster**: Also referred to generically as peripheral, this is a role where a Bluetooth Low Energy device broadcasts/advertises information packets.
    - **Observer**: Also referred to generically as central, this is a role where a Bluetooth Low Energy device listens for the packets and then decides to initiate a connection, or not, depending on the use case.
- **Generic Attribute Profile** (**GATT**): This defines how data or *attributes* are formatted, packaged, and sent across connected devices according to its described rules. Similar to GAP, there are certain roles that interacting devices can adopt:
    - **Client**: This typically sends a request to the GATT server. The client can read and/or write attributes/data found on the server.
    - **Server**: One of the main roles of the server is to store attributes/data. Once the client makes a request, the server must make the attributes/data available.
- **Attribute Protocol**: This defines rules for accessing attributes/data on a device. A GATT profile is built on top of the attribute protocol. Although GATT implements the client server roles, these are *defined* by the **Attribute Protocol**. This protocol also *defines* the fact that data on a server will be arranged in the form of *attributes* each of which will have:
    - A 16-bit attribute handle
    - A UUID
    - A set of permissions
    - A value

Next, the protocol also defines various read and write operations for attributes also known as ATT operations:

- **Read Operations**
- **Write Operations**: These are of type *Write Requests with Response* (write to an attribute and expect a response), *Write* (write without expecting acknowledgement), *Signed Write* (similar to write but uses a signature to authenticate the data)
- **Indications**: These are asynchronous notification operations initiated by the server for the client. This is initiated if the client has subscribed to the updates of attribute values. It requires an acknowledgement from the client.
- **Notifications**: are similar to an indication. The only difference is that they do not require an acknowledgement from the client.

All in all, **Attribute Protocol** is just a set of rules related to accessing data. Don't worry if you don't understand the significance of it at this stage. We will be covering the significance of these characteristics/attributes and related operations in the upcoming sections:

- **Security Manager Protocol**: This defines rules regarding authentication processes such as pairing
- **Logical Link Controller and Adaptation Protocol (L2CAP)**: This defines the following rules:
    - Fragmentation and defragmentation of application data
    - Multiplexing and demultiplexing of multiple channels over a shared logical link

The **Host** layer defines three very important specifications, that is, characteristics, services, and profiles, which help Bluetooth Low Energy devices to discover, identify, and talk to each other.

It really can't be stressed enough that a thorough understanding of these three specifications is absolutely imperative to design robust Bluetooth Low Energy oriented applications. We will go over each of these in detail, right after we have briefly touched on the controller layer.

Controller

Simply speaking, the controller is the actual Bluetooth chip or hardware, which facilitates transmission and receipt of Bluetooth signals:

Figure 10: TI CC2540 Bluetooth Low Energy SoC

It consists of the **Link Layer** and the **Physical Layer**. As the name already suggests, the **Physical layer** consists of all the complex analog circuits, which transmit and receive the digital data over the air. The **Link Layer**, on the other hand, is responsible for scanning, advertising, creating, and maintaining links (connections) between devices. The link layer can have five states: **Standby**, **Advertising**, **Scanning**, **Initiating**, and **Connection** (master-slave):

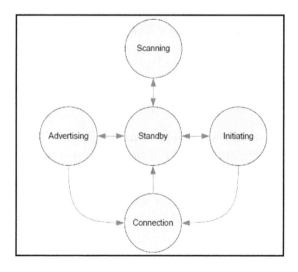

Figure 11: Link Layer States, source: www.bluetooth.com

Delving deeper into the three main pillars of the Bluetooth Low Energy technology should have already given you an idea of what lies under the hood. Now, as promised, let's discuss the important specifications defined by the **Host** layer, starting with profiles.

Profiles

Profile, in a generic sense as a verb, means *to describe,* and that is what actually Bluetooth Low Energy Profiles are. In a nutshell, A Bluetooth Low Energy Profile is a description of the behavior of a Bluetooth Low Energy device, and it is also an answer to questions like "What is the purpose of this device?" or "What can this device do?"

Perhaps, a conversation between a company executive and the software development team lead revolving around a Bluetooth Low Energy device will give you an idea of the importance of profiles for Bluetooth Low Energy devices:

Healthcare Company Executive: *"We want to roll out a new series of health devices for recording and monitoring a user's blood pressure"*

Software Development Lead: *"Ok, sure. Do you have some specifics in mind about this device?"*

Healthcare Company Executive: *"Yes, this will be a small handheld device which can diagnose, record user's blood pressure and send the readings to an app installed on the user's smartphone. The app will then upload the data to our servers to be made available to the doctor for diagnosis."*

Software Development Lead: *"Since this is an on-demand connectivity device; that is, the user only has to connect to the smartphone to transfer the data; hence this can be built into a low power consumption device which uses Bluetooth Low Energy as a mode of communication with the smartphone. Also, the device will support Blood Pressure Profile to be recognized as a healthcare device, which can process blood pressure data."*

After the decision committee has reached a conclusion:

Software Development Lead to Developers: *"Our company is rolling out a Bluetooth Low Energy based medical device supporting Blood Pressure Profile and we need to write an app for that. More details in tomorrow's meeting. Please come prepared for the meeting."*

Our seasoned developer, developing a newer profile, will now head over to the Bluetooth SIG website to read the specification about the Blood Pressure Profile in preparation for the upcoming meeting.

For more information regarding profiles at Bluetooth SIG visit: `https://www.bluetooth.com/specifications/adopted-specifications#gattspec` and for Blood Pressure Profile visit: `https://goo.gl/jVcB0n`.

This is a very real example of an ideal IoT+BLE use case and devices like these already exist fulfilling similar use cases.

 To know more about a popular blood pressure meter visit: `http://www.welltec-usa.com/welltec-idt-products-blood-pressure-BLE.html`. Also, a popular blood glucose meter can be found at: `https://www.accu-chek.com/meters/aviva-connect-meter`.

The preceding discussion might already have given you some vague idea regarding what a profile actually is and how it matters for a Bluetooth Low Energy device. To solidify it to some extent, here is a popular visualization of a profile:

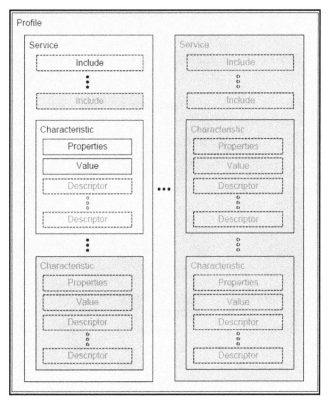

Figure 12: Bluetooth Low Energy Profile

As the diagram shows, the profile dictates what services each profile hosts and, before delving deeper into that, we would request you please go over the Blood Pressure Profile description document available at the link provided previously, since, not only will it give you a better understanding of what we just discussed, but it will also be very helpful in what we are about to discuss. Don't worry if you don't understand everything there (and in the preceding diagram) at once, as we will be delving much deeper into services and other acronyms, which might be puzzling you at this stage.

Going over the Blood Pressure Profile description document, a few things would have jumped out at you right off the bat:

- Blood Pressure Profile requires a GATT profile
- It defines two roles GATT Server (Sensor) and GATT Client (collector)

If you recall, this is exactly what we discussed when we went over the **Host** layer and briefly touched upon the role of the GATT profile. We are now seeing glucose profile building upon GATT and defining individual device roles for a connection to be established between two devices.

The **Profile** document also dictates what kind of services the sensor will contain by mentioning the following:

- The blood pressure sensor will instantiate one, and only one, blood pressure service
- The blood pressure sensor will instantiate the device information service

That exactly maps up if you look closely at the **Profile** diagram. The Blood Pressure Profile is already dictating the kind of services it will contain. And this brings us to the question, "What exactly are Services?", which will be our next topic of discussion.

Services

Extending further from the previous section, we saw that the GATT profile imposes a client–server architecture to facilitate the communication between Bluetooth Low Energy devices (the sensor and the collector) and Bluetooth Low Energy technology. Following a service-oriented architecture, the blood pressure sensor (or any other Bluetooth Low Energy device playing a GATT Server role) exposes some services.

Remember, how we compared Bluetooth Low Energy to a very intelligent database in the previous section, and that is exactly what is happening here. The primary reason for the existence of a blood pressure device sensor (or any other Bluetooth Low Energy sensor/device) is extremely simple. It measures the correct data (blood pressure levels in this case), stores it, and then makes the data available when requested by a client. A service is a wrapper on top of this data (this data is also known as *characteristics* and more on characteristics later). Similar kinds of data or characteristics are bundled together in a single service. This is a key factor in understanding the design of services, which exist to bundle similar kinds of data together. Perhaps an example will provide further clarity to this. The Blood Pressure Profile indicated the existence of two kinds of services:

- **Blood Pressure Service**: This consists of **Blood Pressure Measurement** data/characteristics
- **Device Information Service**: This consists of device data (**Manufacturer Name, Model Number, Serial Number**, and **Hardware Revision**):

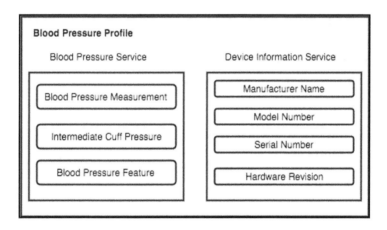

Figure 13: Services in a Blood Pressure Profile

Did you notice how each service consists of different kinds of data, which is similarly pertaining to itself? If you want to get blood pressure data, you should go and interrogate the blood pressure service and if you need information about the device itself, then you should go and talk to the device service. This is the primary reason for the existence of services. We had already established in the previous section that a profile can have multiple services. Like Bluetooth profiles, the Bluetooth SIG defines a number of official services.

 Visit `https://www.bluetooth.com/specifications/gatt/services` for more insight on service definitions by bluetooth SIG.

Each official service is assigned a unique 16-bit UUID so that it can distinguish itself from others; for example, a blood pressure service has a UUID of 0x1810 and a device information service has a UUID of 0x180A. You can also write your own custom service for a specific purpose, but then it will need to have a 128-bit custom UUID.

Once again, I will strongly advise you to go over the relevant documentation of **Blood Pressure Service** and **Device Information Service**. Not only will this be very helpful in the discussion ahead, it will also clarify the information indicated in the preceding diagram.

For further reading on **Blood Pressure Service,** please visit: `https://www.bluetooth.com/specifications/gatt/viewer?attributeXmlFile=org.bluetooth.service.blood_pressure.xml`. For further reading on **Device Information Service,** please visit: `https://www.bluetooth.com/specifications/gatt/viewer?attributeXmlFile=org.bluetooth.service.device_information.xml`

The documents outline what *characteristics* each of the services contain or what information can be found on interrogating relevant services. For example, the blood pressure service contains three distinct characteristics:

- **Blood Pressure Measurement**
- **Intermediate Cuff Pressure**
- **Blood Pressure Feature**

The documentation also indicates what kind of data each characteristic holds; for example, the **Blood Pressure Feature** characteristic is used to describe the supported features of the blood pressure sensor. And by that, we have already started touching base on *characteristics* which deserve a topic of their own.

Characteristics

Characteristics are the lowest and the most important echelon of the Bluetooth Low Energy technology. Encapsulated by a related service, these are the actual state variables, each of which stores a single piece of relevant measurement and information data:

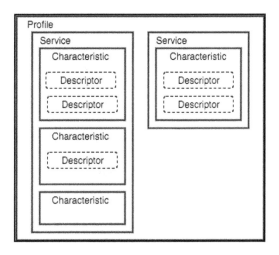

Figure 14: Relationship of Characteristics, Service, and Profile

Just like services, these have a UUID, which can be 16-bit or 128-bit based, depending on whether a characteristic has a standard or custom definition. For example, the blood glucose measurement characteristic has a UUID of 0x2A35. Also, just like services, a manufacturer is free to define custom characteristics of only his/her software, but to facilitate maximum interoperability between Bluetooth Low Energy devices, it is always better to follow the definition of standard characteristics. Bluetooth SIG defines a list of standard Bluetooth Low Energy characteristics here.

To get a list of standard Bluetooth Low Energy characteristics, visit
`https://www.bluetooth.com/specifications/gatt/characteristics`.

It is worthwhile taking a look at the collection of characteristics exposed by the **Blood Pressure Service**.

To know more about characteristics and their descriptors in a blood pressure measurement service, visit `https://www.bluetooth.com/specifications/gatt/viewer?attributeXmlFile=org.bluetooth.service.blood_pressure.xml`.

Remember how we previously discussed that we can abstract Bluetooth Low Energy as an intelligent database. To build all that intelligence, characteristics bundle much more than a single value. Although the value is of prime importance, it is important to understand what makes this intelligent database magical.

Each characteristic as a whole comprises the following:

- **Characteristic declaration**: The characteristic declaration is an important part of a characteristic as it contains the UUID and properties of a characteristic. The properties of a characteristic are 8-bits lined together, which determine how the value of the characteristic can be used and how the descriptors can be accessed. You should already have seen the properties associated with each characteristic of the Blood Pressure Profile service by visiting the preceding link. We discuss the relevance of each of these properties as follows:
  - **Read**: If this bit is set, then it means that clients are allowed to read this characteristic's value.
  - **Write**: If this bit is set, then it means that clients are allowed to write (and receive a response) to this characteristic's value.
  - **Write without response**: If this bit is set, then it means that clients are allowed to write (without response) to this characteristic's value.
  - **Signed Write**: If this bit is set, then it means that clients are allowed to do a signed write to this characteristic's value.
  - **Notify**: One of the important ones. If set then the server will asynchronously notify the client whenever the value of the characteristic gets updated on the server. We will discuss this more in the next section. Also, if set, then the client configuration descriptor will exist. We shall discuss descriptors in detail shortly.
  - **Indicate**: Similar to notify, the only difference is that an indication requires an acknowledgement from the client. We will discuss this more in the next section. Also, if set, then the client configuration descriptor will exist. We shall discuss descriptors in detail shortly.
  - **Write auxiliaries**: If set, then the client can write to the characteristic user description descriptor.
  - **Broadcast**: If this bit is set, then it means that the value of this characteristic will be broadcasted, that is, placed in advertising packets.
  - **Extended properties**: Is set, then additional properties are defined in the characteristic extended properties descriptor, which also means that the characteristic extended properties descriptor shall exist. We shall discuss descriptors in detail shortly.

These properties are essentially the guidelines for how clients can interact with this characteristic and also, how they can subscribe (listen) to indications and/or notifications of this characteristic. We will see how the indications and notifications can be enabled in the next section.

- **Characteristic Value**: This is self-explanatory. You can already see how the measurement data is packaged for a blood pressure measurement characteristic at the link provided in the upcoming information box.

To know more about packaging of data in a blood pressure measurement visit `https://www.bluetooth.com/specifications/gatt/viewer?attributeXmlFile=org.bluetooth.characteristic.blood_pressure_measurement.xml`.

- **Characteristic Descriptor**: Each characteristic can be followed by one or more descriptors. Descriptors contain more information regarding a characteristic and its value. Just like services and characteristics (and you might have already guessed it here), these can either have a standard definition or a custom definition. To help clarify, we shall discuss some standard descriptors defined by GATT.

For a list of GATT descriptors, you can proceed to visit `https://www.bluetooth.com/specifications/gatt/descriptors`.

- **Client Characteristic Configuration Descriptor (CCCD)**: This is one of the most important and most commonly used descriptors. This descriptor is used when you need to configure (enable/disable) indications or notifications for the characteristic. It is this descriptor that makes our *so-called database* so intelligent. By correctly configuring it for a characteristic, a client (possibly your app J) can expect to be dynamically notified whenever the characteristic updates its value on the GATT Server (a Bluetooth Low Energy sensor such as a blood pressure or a blood glucose meter). The blood pressure measurement characteristic includes a client characteristic configuration descriptor.

For an insight into descriptors included in a blood pressure measurement visit `https://www.bluetooth.com/specifications/gatt/viewer?attributeXmlFile=org.bluetooth.service.blood_pressure.xml`.

For CCCD specification details included in a blood pressure measurement visit `https://www.bluetooth.com/specifications/gatt/viewer?attributeXmlFile=org.bluetooth.descriptor.gatt.client_characteristic_configuration.xml`.

- **Characteristic User Description Descriptor**: As the name already suggests, this descriptor contains a human-readable string that describes the characteristic's value, which also can be directly presented to the user.

The specification for a characteristic user description descriptor is available at `https://www.bluetooth.com/specifications/gatt/viewer?attributeXmlFile=org.bluetooth.descriptor.gatt.characteristic_user_description.xml`.

- **Extended Properties Descriptor**: If this is present, it contains information about extended properties.

The specification for a extended properties descriptor is available at `https://www.bluetooth.com/specifications/gatt/viewer?attributeXmlFile=org.bluetooth.descriptor.gatt.characteristic_extended_properties.xml`.

Starting with Profiles, we finally covered the lowermost echelon of the Bluetooth Low Energy communication, the characteristic. We saw that it is not just as simple as reading and writing to/from a characteristic. We also touched upon the *magic* of indications and notifications upon which the whole Bluetooth Low Energy communication relies heavily and, hence, they deserve a topic of their own.

Indications and Notifications

We briefly touched upon indications and notifications in the previous section. Indications and notifications basically are server (GATT) side updates to a client. A client has to configure Indications and Notifications for a characteristic's value through its client characteristic configuration descriptor to get notified every time a characteristic's value gets updated on the server:

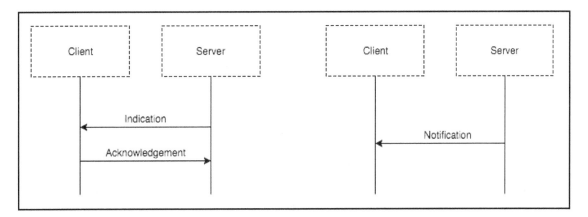

Figure 15: Indications versus notifications

As shown in the preceding figure:

- **Indications**: They need to be acknowledged by the client. The server does not send the next indication until it gets the acknowledgement back from the client. Hence communication via indications is slower.
- **Notifications**: They do not need to be acknowledged by the client. Hence, communication via notifications is faster.

Indications and Notifications are a very important mechanism for receiving server-side data probably due to the fact that they are the *only* and fastest mechanism for receiving asynchronous server-side updates. Since Bluetooth Low Energy was designed to be energy efficient, this asynchronous method of receiving updates prevents continuous polling of the server by the client and, hence, is a huge energy saver too.

Bluetooth 5, Meshes, and Beacons

The retail market for *connected things* is projected to have a worth of 53.75 billion by 2022 and Bluetooth Low Energy is forecast to witness a substantial growth with a CAGR of over 25% during the forecast period.

 For more extensive reading on the study conducted on the growth of the retail market of connected things, visit `https://iotbusinessnews.com/ 2016/03/16/57411-connected-retail-market-worth-53-75-billion- usd-by-2022/`.

In other words, this makes Bluetooth Low Energy a significant driver for this forecast growth and technology to be taken seriously. Bluetooth SIG is leaving no stone unturned to make the existing Bluetooth Low Energy technology a better fit for IoT Applications. The SIG recently finalized and released the specification for Bluetooth 5, which takes the existing technology to the next level by enabling quadrupled range, twice the speed and increasing the data broadcasting capacity by 800%. These new features are specifically focused on Internet of Things technology.

 You can find the press release by SIG (Bluetooth Special Interest Group) for Bluetooth 5 at `https://www.bluetooth.com/news/pressreleases/ 2016/06/16/-bluetooth5-quadruples-rangedoubles-speedincreases- data-broadcasting-capacity-by-800`.

However, MCUs supporting Bluetooth Low Energy 5 like the one shown here are already available:

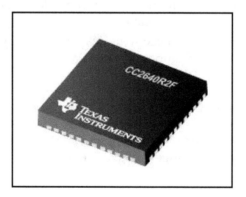

Figure 16: CC2640R2F MCU supporting Bluetooth Low Energy 5

Bluetooth 5 is a new standard, which has been rolled out very recently (from the end of 2016 to the beginning of 2017). For the consumers, it may take some time to *feel* the difference between the older Bluetooth Low Energy 4.2 versus the Bluetooth Low Energy 5 as various device manufacturers will adopt this standard and manufacture Bluetooth Low Energy 5 compatible devices, which will then hit the market and eventually end up in the hands of the consumers. As of the writing of this book, Samsung has already taken the lead and has released Galaxy S8 worldwide during the period towards the end of April and beginning of May 2017, which is the first smartphone to support and an early adopter of Bluetooth Low Energy 5. However, another key update, which is not immediately included in the Bluetooth Low Energy 5 standard is the specification for Mesh Networking. It is still said to be in works and probably will arrive early next year. This update for Bluetooth Low Energy is crucial for the IoT paradigm as it can enable data to be transferred across even greater distances just via Bluetooth Low Energy nodes/hubs. We shall briefly touch upon Mesh Networking to see how this is possible.

Traditional Bluetooth Low Energy network topology looks something similar to the star topology such as shown in the following diagram:

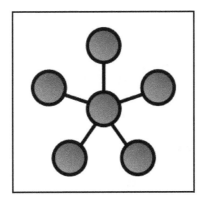

Figure 17: A traditional Bluetooth Low Energy network star topology; source: www.wikipedia.com

Here, one device acts as the server and others access information (characteristics) from the server, if and when required. It goes without saying that this is the traditional way of communication, and it limits the networking capabilities in terms of the following:

- Limited range/distance of data transfer
- Nodes are not directly connected, all data goes through a central device (server)
- Single point of failure, if the server fails everything else fails too

The preceding factors mentioned can severely limit an IoT-based solution.

The solution to this is the eagerly awaited mesh networking update, intended to transforming each individual Bluetooth Low Energy node to a hub, where the node/hub can also transfer data to the nearby devices. This will change the network topology from a traditional star network to a Mesh as shown as follows:

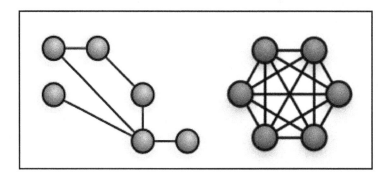

Figure 18: A mesh topology; source: www.wikipedia.com

This means each node of the network can accept and forward data to a neighboring node, allowing a network to scale more easily by just adding new nodes. A mesh network exhibits the following characteristics:

- **Self Forming/Organising**: As soon as a new node joins the network, all its adjacent nodes are notified so that an optimized path can be configured dynamically for the data packets.
- **Self Healing**: If one node fails in the network then surrounding nodes immediately become aware of this and an optimized path is configured dynamically for the remaining data packets. A single node cannot cause the failure of the complete network. The network continues to function without any downtime as long as the density of the devices is sufficient to keep the communication ongoing.
- **Self Optimization**: The network can self-optimize itself to have as large a coverage as possible.

Another pre-existing piece of hardware technology, which is greatly going to benefit with Bluetooth Low Energy 5 is Beacons. Beacons are small sized, Bluetooth Low Energy devices which broadcast information:

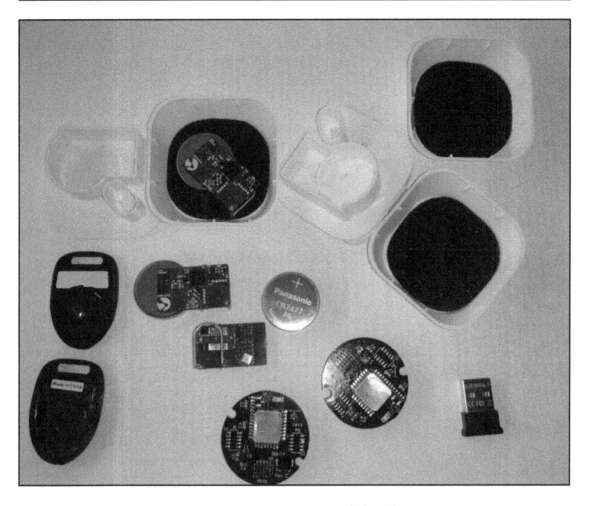

Figure 19: Beacons from various vendors; source: www.wikipedia.com

Bluetooth Low Energy Beacons are primarily used for proximity broadcasting or advertising. A very popular use case of beacons is to broadcast/advertise contextual information to nearby smartphones and handheld devices, which support Bluetooth Low Energy, in close proximity. The context of the information can be bus updates on a bus stop, new products in a store, or special delicacies available at a restaurant.

The other uses of Beacons include:

- **Indoor Navigation**: Since GPS does not work indoors, Bluetooth Low Energy can be used for indoor navigation by placing beacons at strategic places in a closed space (houses/offices)
- **Tracking Things**: Bluetooth Low Energy based Beacons/tags can be attached as trackers to things that are more prone to getting lost, such as keys. These items can then be monitored via a smartphone app
- **Personal Monitoring**: Monitoring patients, the elderly, and toddlers inside a home

There are already various preprogrammed beacons and respective development kits available in the market.

 For an insight about Estimote Beacons, please visit `https://estimote.com/`.

However, later in the course of this book, we will take the road less traveled and create a beacon of our own using a Raspberry Pi. Also, we shall discuss the two primary Beacon protocols namely, Eddystone and iBeacon.

Summary

Phew! We covered a lot of ground in this chapter, which although substantial is still just the tip of the iceberg. However, I feel pretty confident in saying that you as a reader should now be familiar with the answers to the following questions, which we asked before starting this chapter:

- Why was Bluetooth Low Energy designed or what is the need for Bluetooth Low Energy?
- What are the differences between Bluetooth Low Energy and Bluetooth Classic?
- What does the architecture of Bluetooth Low Energy look like?

Apart from delving deeper to answer these questions, we also briefly touched upon the advent of the latest Bluetooth Low Energy 5 specification and how it is going to help IoT to reach new levels of connectivity and data exchange between devices. Furthermore, we also scratched the surface of Mesh Networking and Beacons.

With all this theory under our belt, we are now going to apply it to gain hands-on knowledge over the course of this book. Going ahead, we will be setting up our development environment, sniffing a fit-bit device, brewing our very own homemade beacons, designing a personnel tracking system using iTags, and we'll then bring it all together by building a complete warehouse monitoring system. So put on your seat belts, here we go.

2
Setting Up

In theory, there is no difference between theory and practice. In practice, there is.

- Anonymous

We established quite a theoretical foundation in the last chapter by covering the pillars on which Bluetooth Low Energy is designed upon. In this chapter, we will be setting up our development environment, which will help us to put all that theory into practice.

We will eventually set up our development environment by covering the following topics:

- Introduction to Bluetooth Low Energy Sensors
- Setting Up Your System to Write Android Applications
- Setting Up Your System to Write iOS Applications
- Configuring the Firebase Cloud Backend
- Introduction to Raspberry Pi
- Introduction to GitHub

Introduction to Bluetooth Low Energy Sensors

Almost every BLE device that you will be interacting with in the real world and during the course of this book, will be a sensor that senses and stores data, waiting to be read. For example, a Fitbit senses heart rate, quality of sleep, and the number of steps walked. We will be interacting with a Fitbit device in the next chapter to understand how it stores the sensed data and how it makes that data available to us:

Figure 1: A Fitbit charge 2 device; source: www.fitbit.com

Temperature and humidity sensors can also use Bluetooth Low Energy as their communication protocol to transfer data to handheld devices or hubs. We will be creating an IoT + BLE solution for one such use case involving temperature and humidity sensors in `Chapter 6`, *Weather Monitoring Using BLE in Warehouses*:

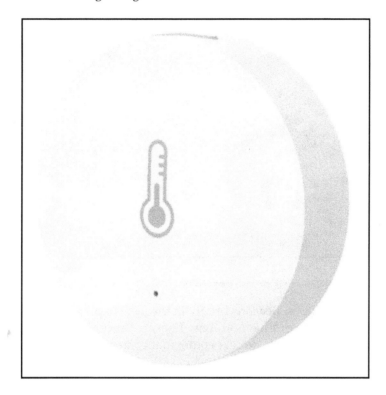

Figure 2: Temperature and humidity sensor by Xiaomi; source: www.Xiaomi.com

Bluetooth Low Energy sensors can also be used to sense the approximate location (mainly distance) of a person or thing. Such types of sensors are mostly used in iTags, which are small tags that can be attached to car/home keys or maybe kept in the pockets of kids/infants for better monitoring. We will look into how personal monitoring with an iTag works in more detail in `Chapter 4`, *Designing a Personnel Tracking System*:

Figure 3: An iTag with open battery compartment; source: `blog.banggood.com`

We have already touched upon Beacons briefly in the last chapter. Beacons still remain one of the most popular use cases of Bluetooth Low Energy. Beacons, such as estimotes, can be used to sense human presence and deliver contextual content:

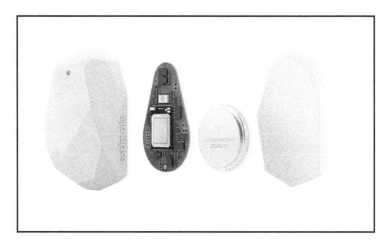

Figure 4: An estimote and its internals

For example, the Guggenheim Museum in New York delivers relevant content to your smartphone depending on which artwork you are closest to.

 To learn how Beacons are being utilized by the Guggenheim Museum in New York city, visit `http://blog.estimote.com/post/157200820650/the-icon-of-modern-art-puts-estimote-beacons-on`.

At a fundamental level, almost all the sensors we will be introducing and using will have a similar way of working, as outlined in the following steps:

- **Record relevant data**: Heart Rate Sensors record heart rate, Blood Pressure Sensors record blood pressure, Beacons record and send out pre-recorded contextual data, for example.
- **Expose the recorded data via standard services and characteristics**: Ideally, a Heart Rate Sensor will be built on top of a Heart Rate Profile and will expose the standard heart rate service, which will have characteristics corresponding to heart rate measurement.
- **Make data available to the client devices**: Clients can read the relevant characteristics from a service and configure the CCCD to receive indications and notifications regarding relevant data.

There is so much more to learn about these sensors, whose primary job is to make relevant data available to Bluetooth Low Energy clients. Now let's go ahead and gear up to write up our very own apps to interact with these wonderful sensors.

Setting Up Your System to Write Android Applications

For those who came late, here is a little bit of history on Android.

Android is a mobile operating system initially developed by Google. The initial release of Android happened on September 23, 2008. Alongside the release, Google also took the initiative to form the **Open Handset Alliance** (**OHA**), which is a group of 84 companies including Sony, Dell, Samsung Electronics, HTC, and Motorola to name a few. Note that Android was and is a platform, and the primary purpose of the OHA was to develop open standards for mobile devices and promote the Android platform.

For more information about the Android operating system, visit `https://www.android.com/`.

Looking at the historical timeline of Android releases, you will realize that Android has really come a long way since 2008:

Code name	Version number	Initial release date	API level
(No codename)[4]	1.0	September 23, 2008	1
(Internally known as "Petit Four")[4]	1.1	February 9, 2009	2
Cupcake	1.5	April 27, 2009	3
Donut[5]	1.6	September 15, 2009	4
Eclair[6]	2.0–2.1	October 26, 2009	5–7
Froyo[7]	2.2–2.2.3	May 20, 2010	8
Gingerbread[8]	2.3–2.3.7	December 6, 2010	9–10
Honeycomb[9]	3.0–3.2.6	February 22, 2011	11–13
Ice Cream Sandwich[10]	4.0–4.0.4	October 18, 2011	14–15
Jelly Bean[11]	4.1–4.3.1	July 9, 2012	16–18
KitKat[12]	4.4–4.4.4	October 31, 2013	19
Lollipop[14]	5.0–5.1.1	November 12, 2014	21–22
Marshmallow[15]	6.0–6.0.1	October 5, 2015	23
Nougat[16]	**7.0–7.1.2**	**August 22, 2016**	**24–25**
O	*8.0*	TBA	*26*

Figure 5: Android version history timeline; source: `www.wikipedia.com`

Fun fact—All of the code names for Android flavors are in reference to sweets and the first letter of each flavor name follows an alphabetical order with respect to the next one.

Accompanying Android and the OHA, the Google Play Store was also launched where developers can launch their apps written for the Android platform. Google Play Store also allows developers to collect insightful statistics about their apps and devices active on the play store. In fact, Google itself uses the play store to gather insightful data regarding Android market share and statistics, as shown below:

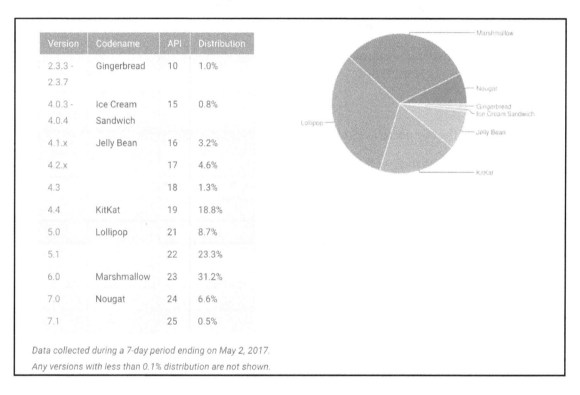

Version	Codename	API	Distribution
2.3.3 - 2.3.7	Gingerbread	10	1.0%
4.0.3 - 4.0.4	Ice Cream Sandwich	15	0.8%
4.1.x	Jelly Bean	16	3.2%
4.2.x		17	4.6%
4.3		18	1.3%
4.4	KitKat	19	18.8%
5.0	Lollipop	21	8.7%
5.1		22	23.3%
6.0	Marshmallow	23	31.2%
7.0	Nougat	24	6.6%
7.1		25	0.5%

Data collected during a 7-day period ending on May 2, 2017.
Any versions with less than 0.1% distribution are not shown.

Figure 6: Insights collected from Google play store; source: developer.android.com

From time to time, Google publishes updated Play Store statistics.

For the latest Play Store statistics visit https://developer.android.com/about/dashboards/index.html.

An important observation from the data presented above is the fact that Marshmallow, Lollipop, and Kitkat are the dominant releases on the Play Store. This can already help you in deciding the minimum sdk version for your next popular app. We will understand the significance of the minimum sdk version as soon as we download Android Studio, which is the default and officially supported IDE for Android development by Google. Navigate to the following link, you should see a **DOWNLOAD ANDROID STUDIO** button depending on your operating system (Windows, Mac, or Linux), and start the download.

 To download Android Studio, visit `https://developer.android.com/studio/index.html`.

The following are the supported OS versions for Android development:

- Microsoft® Windows® 7/8/10 (32- or 64-bit)
- Mac® OS X® 10.10 (Yosemite) or higher, up to 10.12 (Sierra)
- Linux: GNOME or KDE desktop

A detailed list of requirements including RAM and hard disk requirements is available here under system requirements.

 To get information about system requirements for Android development machines, visit `https://developer.android.com/studio/index.html`.

We'll be covering the development setup for Mac OS here as that corresponds to my personal development environment.

 Having a Mac-based development environment also helps, since you can then develop for both Android and iOS on a single system.

But don't let that scare you, there are plenty of tutorials available out there to guide you with the setup for Windows and Linux too. One such comprehensive tutorial is mentioned next.

 For additional help in setting up the Android development environment for Mac, Windows, and Linux visit `http://www.androidcentral.com/installing-android-sdk-windows-mac-and-linux-tutorial`.

Android Studio requires a working version of Java to operate. On a Mac, you need not do anything special as Java is preinstalled (unless you uninstalled it and in that case you can head over to the Oracle website mentioned as follows to download and install the appropriate Java (32/64 bit) for your system).

 You can check whether Java is installed on your system or not by running the `java -version` command on terminal on a Mac machine.

Your copy of Android Studio should have finished downloading by now. Perform the following steps to set up the Android development environment and create a `Hello World` program. Successful execution of this will eventually prove that our setup is correct:

1. Double-click on the downloaded `.dmg` file and in the shown dialog, copy the Android Studio executable to the `Applications` directory.
2. After copying, click on the icon and start the set up, you should be immediately prompted with a dialog to import your previous settings. I am assuming that you did not have a previous version of Android Studio installed and hence would not like to import previous settings, therefore choose the option that states so.
3. After that, it is pretty much straightforward, by clicking on **Next** and choosing a **Standard** installation.

If everything goes well, you should be presented with the Android Studio welcome screen as follows:

Figure 7: Android Studio welcome screen

And, as they say, well begun is half done.

Now we shall go ahead and write our first `Hello World` program on Android:

 Fun fact—in the programming jargon, `Hello World` means success.

1. Click on the **Start a new Android Studio project** on the Android Studio welcome screen.

2. This will bring up a dialog where you can choose your project name, package name, and the location of the project on your hard drive, which should be pre-populated.

3. After naming your application, click on **Next**, which will bring you to the selection of minimum sdk.

If you remember we ran into the concept of **minimum sdk version** earlier, and now we will elaborate on it. Minimum SDK refers to the minimum version of Android SDK that an application supports and is all about backward compatibility. A lower value for the minimum sdk version ensures more backwards compatibility with older Android releases, but also requires more effort towards development/coding because some API(s) will be deprecated and not used in newer versions of Android, while others will be new and unavailable in older versions. You will need to make a balanced choice here and to help you with this there is a **Help Me Choose** button on this screen, which at the time of writing this book in May 2017, showed this visual:

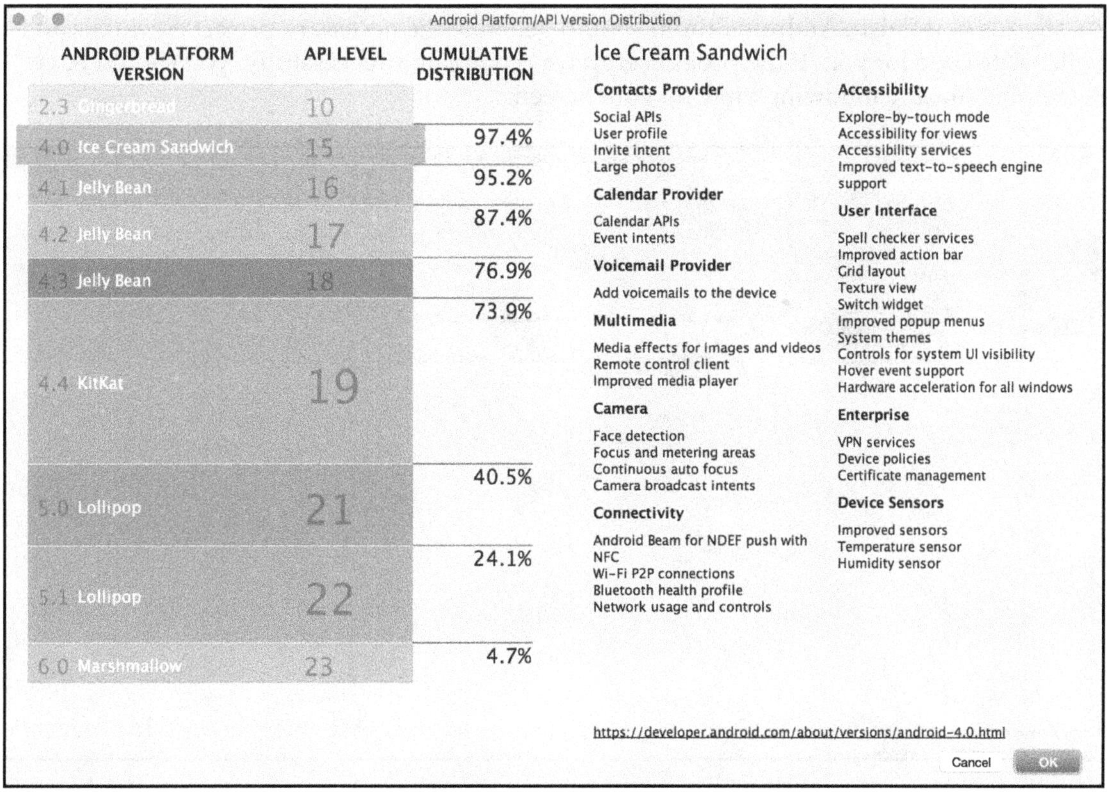

Figure 8: Android Platform Version Distribution

Using the data collected through Google Play Store statistics, Android Studio is helping you make a choice by suggesting Android 4.0, API level 15, which stands at a whopping 97.4% distribution and also looks like a lucrative choice:

1. We will go ahead with this and choose it as our minimum supported SDK (for now).
2. Clicking on **Next** brings you to the choice of activities for your application.

 For simplicity of this and this app only, an Activity is a screen. For more information about an Android Activity, visit `https://developer.` `android.com/reference/android/app/Activity.html`.

3. Choose an **Empty Activity** and click on N**ext**, which should bring you toward naming your activity.
4. Keep the default values filled in and finish the process.

As soon as you finish, Android Studio should generate the necessary project essentials and boilerplate code for you. If the project setup was completed successfully, you should have something like the following view on your screen:

Figure 9: Initial view of the starter project in Android Studio

Let's take a minute to understand the project structure that was generated. In the left pane is the project structure and in the right pane are the details of the file that is currently selected. The following are the most important files/directories:

- `AndroidManifest.xml`: This provides the necessary information about the app to the Android system
- Source files: The Android apps are primarily programmed in Java. The highlighted source file, `MainActivity`, in the preceding screenshot is one such source file, which contains the source code of an Activity.
- `layout`: This is a directory and contains the layout files. Layout files in android consist of UI elements/views defined in xml format. In the preceding screenshot, `activity_main.xml` consists of UI corresponding to `MainActivity`.

Android programming is a pretty vast topic in itself which deserves a book (or a few books) of its own. The Android developer website is one of the best knowledge resources out there for novices and experts alike.

> To gather more knowledge on specific topics related to Android, visit
> `https://developer.android.com/training/index.html`.

Coming back to our Android project, Android Studio has already generated all the boilerplate code for us and to see this in action all you need to do is enable the developer mode on an Android phone, connect the Android phone (we used an LG Nexus 5 running Android 6.0) via USB to the system and press the green play button.

> For troubleshooting and learning more about running Android apps on physical devices in developer mode, please visit - `https://developer.android.com/training/basics/firstapp/running-app.html`

We highly recommend using physical Android and iOS devices throughout the course of this book since we will be dealing with Bluetooth functionality, which is not supported on emulators and simulators. If all goes well, then you should be presented with a screen like the following on your Android device:

Figure 10: Hello World, Android

The preceding screenshot says `Hello World`, which tells us that our Android development environment has been set up successfully.

Setting Up Your System to Write iOS Applications

Just like Android, iOS needs no formal introduction; however, we will go over some key knowledge factors related to it. iOS or iPhone OS is a mobile operating system which was developed by Apple Inc. and first introduced in June 2007 exclusively for Apple devices:

Figure 11: Devices supported by iOS; source: www.macworld.com

Note that one of the biggest differences between Android and iOS is that Apple designed iOS as an *operating system*, which was exclusively designed for Apple hardware. On the other hand, Android took more of a *platform* approach, which dictated a set of requirements and then the phone manufacturers could roll out devices adhering to these requirements. Also, this implies that iOS is closed source whereas Android is open source.

Just like Android, iOS also has a version history starting right from iPhone OS 1 and currently at the time of writing of this book, iOS 10 which was introduced in September 2016:

Version	Release date	Distribution (as of Feb. 2017)	Devices shipped with version
iOS 10	September 13, 2016	79%	iPhone 7, iPhone 7 Plus, iPad (7th generation)
iOS 9	September 16, 2015	16%	iPhone 6S, iPhone 6S Plus, iPhone SE, iPad Pro, iPad Mini 4
iOS 8 and earlier	N/A	5%	N/A

Figure 12: iOS Device Distribution - 1; source: www.wikipedia.com

Also, just as Android has Play Store, Apple has App Store for publishing apps developed for iOS and gathering device and other usage statistics. The latest Apple device statistics (OS version information distribution) collected from App Store by Apple are mentioned in the following figure:

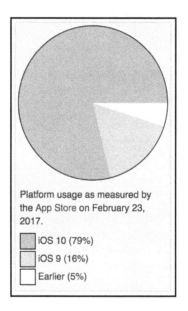

Figure 13: iOS Device Distribution - 2; source: www.wikipedia.com

We already have a brief outline of the operating system now, so let's delve into the development. The following are the requirements for development for iOS:

- A Mac computer with Xcode 7.1 or later installed
- For the best experience, the latest OS X and Xcode releases installed

Please note that compared to Android development, which can be done on all the three major platforms - Mac, Windows, and Linux; iOS development can only be done on the Mac platform.

Once you have your Mac ready, you will need to install Xcode, which is the development IDE (Integrated Development Environment) for iOS Apps. You can download and install the latest version of Xcode from the Mac App Store.

> To download Xcode, visit https://itunes.apple.com/us/app/xcode/id497799835.

Once you have installed Xcode, it can be launched like any other Mac app:

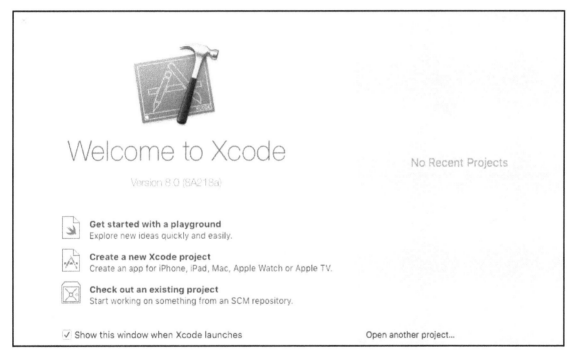

Figure 14: XCode welcome screen

To create a new project, you can select **Create a new Xcode Project** in the welcome window shown in the preceding screenshot. After that, select **Single View Application** on the next screen:

Figure 15: XCode, Project Template Screen

By clicking on **Next** in the preceding screen, you will be presented with the options screen for your new project, fill in the **Product Name** (name of project) and **Organizational Identifier** (package name) on this screen:

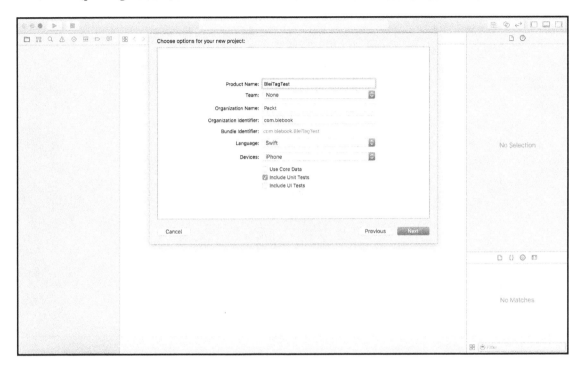

Figure 16: XCode, Project Template Screen

In the preceding screen, also pay close attention to the language selection. Up until 2014, *Objective-C* was the language of development for iOS apps; however, at WWDC 2014, Apple introduced Swift, which is now the new endorsed and recommended language of development for iOS apps.

By clicking on **Next** and specifying the location of the project, you should then be presented with the project view in Xcode for our project:

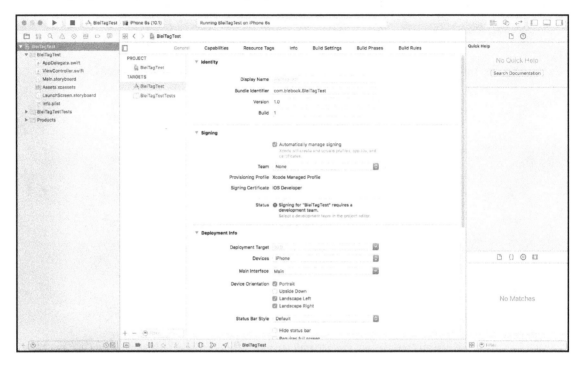

Figure 17: XCode, project view

Let's go briefly over the project structure and points worth considering in the preceding screen:

- **The source files**: Do you notice the `ViewController.swift` file in the preceding screenshot? It is a ViewController source file. ViewControllers are one of the fundamental building blocks of an iOS app and every iOS app has at least a single ViewController. A ViewController is basically the go-between of your UI and the underlying data.
- **User interface**: The **user interface** (**UI**) in iOS apps is primarily designed and contained in storyboards. The UI of this app (which is right now nothing more than a blank screen) is contained in the `Main.Storyboard` file.
- `AppDelegate`: This is the heart or the root of each application in iOS. This is an application delegate, which receives notifications when an app has reached certain important states.

To read more about View Controllers, visit `https://developer.apple.com/library/content/featuredarticles/ViewControllerPGforiPhoneOS/`.

If you look closely in the preceding screenshot, on the right side, you will notice a warning mentioning that **Signing of "BleiTagTest" app requires a development team.** What this essentially means for us is that if we need to deploy our app on actual iOS devices, then we need to provide a signing key and provisioning profile. We can run our app on the simulator without any hurdles however, to run on an actual device, we will still need to complete a few more steps, which will require you to create an Apple ID and generate a signing certificate associated with that ID. The complete process is mentioned at the following link `http://blog.ionic.io/deploying-to-a-device-without-an-apple-developer-account/`.

However, we can already test our setup using the simulator by selecting the appropriate simulator and pressing the play button in the top-left corner of the screen, which should present you with the simulator. Currently only a blank screen is presented as shown below, and this marks the completion of our iOS environment setup:

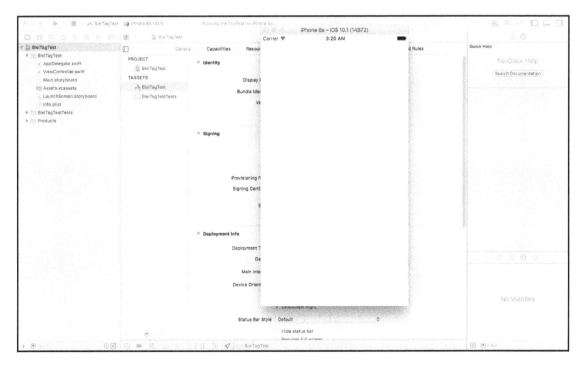

Figure 18: Successful iOS environment setup

Configuring the Firebase Cloud Backend

Firebase, in technical terms, is *backend as a service.* To clarify what this means, let's look at an example: Let's say you would like to write an app, which shows screening times for various movies playing in the city. For this, you will need to store the movie details and the show times in a backend, which can then later be fetched and displayed by various mobile clients. However, you don't want to get into writing a full-fledged server on your own and it would probably be best if you could lay your hands on a pre-cooked solution where you could just store and read your data when needed. This is where Firebase comes in. Firebase is a technology/service that helps developers who want to write apps, which interact with a backend but avoids them creating/programming their own full-fledged backend. This will become clearer as we set up Firebase to use with our Android client.

 Firebase can be used with Android, iOS, OS X, Web, and Unity clients.

Apart from several other functionalities, one of the most well used functionalities of Firebase is real-time data storage and synchronization, where data updated on the cloud is instantly made available to clients:

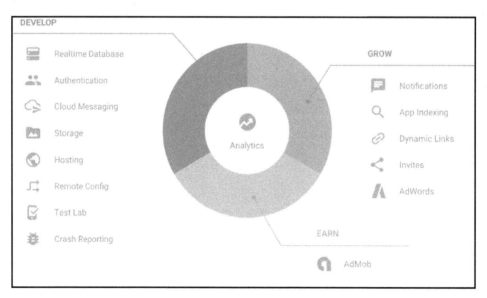

Figure 19: Firebase offerings; source: www.androidhive.info

The Firebase documentation is an excellent place to find guidance on various platforms for its setup.

For in-depth information regarding Firebase, visit `https://firebase.google.com/docs/`.

From Android Studio 2.2 onwards, all the versions of Android Studio come bundled with a Firebase assistant, which makes the setup of Firebase a breeze for Android clients. To set up Firebase for the project we created earlier for the Android setup, open the project in Android Studio and perform the following steps:

1. Before launching the Firebase assistant, we need to install the **Google Support Repository**, version 26 or higher. This can be done by navigating to **Tools | Android | SDK Manager** and clicking on the **SDK Tools** tab. This should bring up the default preferences with **SDK Tools** selected as shown as follows:

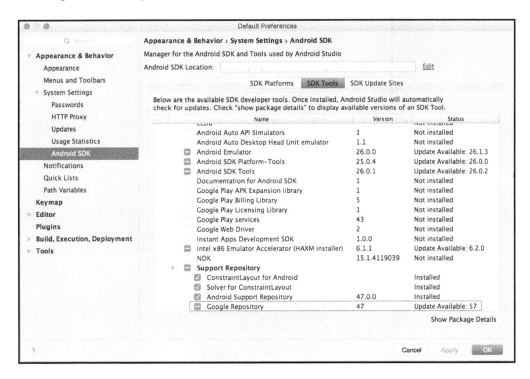

Figure 19.1: Google Repository under SDK Tools

2. Find and check the **Google Repository** checkbox and click on **OK** to install.

3. To launch the Firebase assistant, click on **Tools** and select **Firebase**. This will bring up the **Assistant** window as shown in the following screenshot:

Figure 20: Firebase Assistant bundled with Android Studio

4. Expand on one of the features. Since we will be using **Realtime Database**, we will be expanding that. Click on **Save and retrieve data** after expansion:

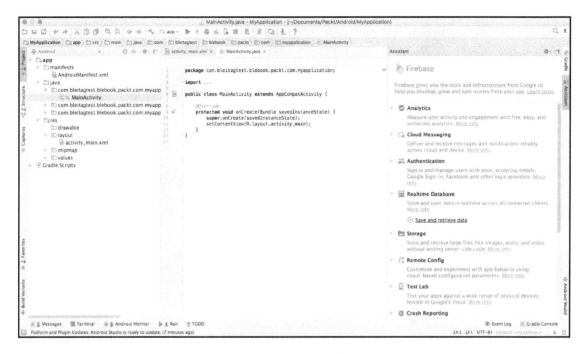

Figure 21: Realtime Database configuration in Android Studio's Firebase Assistance

5. This should bring up the **Save and retrieve data** window. There are five steps outlined in this window (as shown in image as follows):
   - **Connect your app to Firebase**
   - **Add the Realtime Database to your app**
   - **Configure Firebase Database Rules**
   - **Write to your database**
   - **Read from your database**

We shall execute these steps one by one in the given order. Click on **Connect to Firebase** in this window:

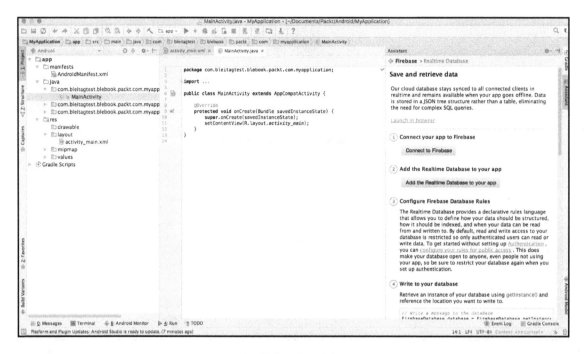

Figure 22: Connecting to Firebase

6. The preceding step should open the default browser on your system and the Firebase connection should ask for your credentials and then to choose an existing project or create a new one.

7. Choose to create a new project and finish up the process by using the default/pre-filled values on the displayed screen. The success of this step is indicated when the green **Connected** text appears under **Connect your app to Firebase**.

8. Now let's move to the next step and add real-time data to our app by clicking on the button that says **Add the Realtime Database to your app**. A prompt comes up when the button is clicked, which displays what changes will be made to the project.

9. Accept the changes and a Gradle Sync will start.

The success of this step is indicated when a green **Dependencies set up correctly** button appears under **Add the Realtime Database to your app**:

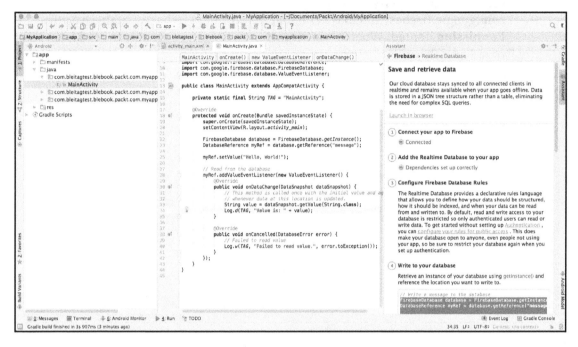

Figure 23: Successful connection and addition of database

Now, just for a little fun, we will skip the third step (**Configure Firebase Database Rules**) and go directly to the fourth (**Write to your database**) and fifth (**Read from your database**) step:

1. Copy the code from the fourth (**Write to your database**) and fifth (**Read from your database**) steps one by one and add it to the `onCreate` method one after the other.
2. Run the app.

3. You will not see anything on the screen, but if you click on **Android Monitor** in Android Studio and take a look at the logs while the app is running, you should see this: **MainActivity: Failed to read value. com.google.firebase.database.DatabaseException: Firebase Database error: Permission denied**. What is happening and why are we unable to read from the remote database?

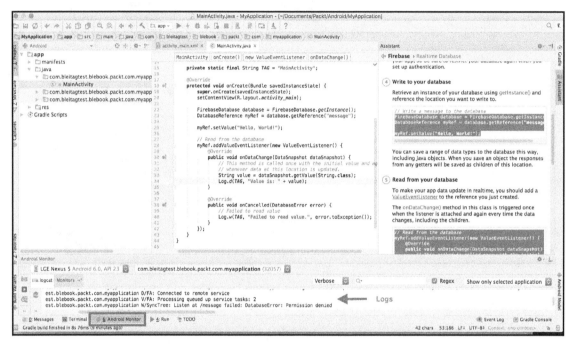

Figure 24: Firebase error by monitoring Android Logs

Well, what just happened is, by default when the assistant initialized a Firebase database for us, it applied some default rules, one of which is not to allow any applications to read the database. We need to change this if we want to read from the database. To do this, we will now need to go to Step 3 in the Firebase Assistant window, which we skipped earlier:

1. Click on **Configure** your rules for public access under *step 3* in the **Assistant** window, which should open Firebase documentation regarding setting up and understanding rules.

2. It is worthwhile going over this documentation to get a better understanding of the Firebase authentication configuration rules.

3. However, you can also directly navigate to `https://console.firebase.google.com/` and click on **MyAppliation** (or whatever the name might be in your context), which should land you on the Firebase console as shown in the following screenshot.

4. Click on **Database** in the left pane and select the **Rules** tab from the list of horizontal tabs:

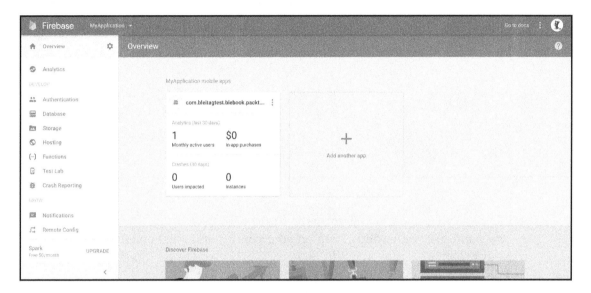

Figure 25: Firebase console

What you should be seeing in front of you is a JSON file signifying rules as key-value pairs:

1. Change the `.read` key from `auth != null` to `true`.
2. Do the same for the `.write` key.
3. Hit the **Publish** button on the top.

Note that this configuration is for demo purposes only and means anyone can read or write to your database. In the real world, your rules will be more advanced and sophisticated than this.

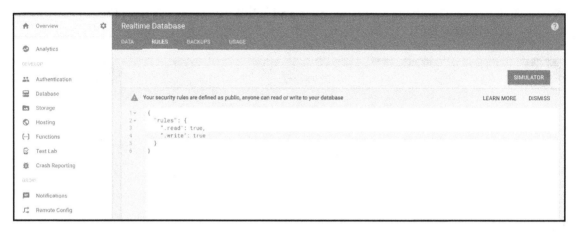

Figure 26: Firebase rules

4. Now switch to the **Data** tab from the **Rules** tab under myapplication-xxxxx (the name may differ depending on your context and what you decided to name your project in Android Studio).
5. Edit and change the message to **Hello Firebase**.

On running the app again and taking a look at the logs in **Android Monitor**, you should see the message **Hello Firebase** popping up, which implies that as soon as the data was updated on the server, Firebase automatically notified your app about the update! Isn't that awesome!

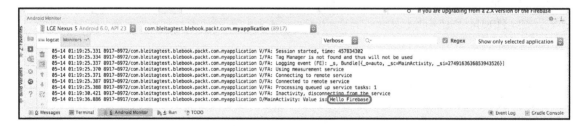

Figure 27: Hello From Firebase

Congratulations! You not only set up Firebase successfully, but also made it talk to an Android Client.

Introduction to Raspberry Pi

In this section, we will be introducing you to Raspberry Pi, which is a completely functional computer built on a single circuit board:

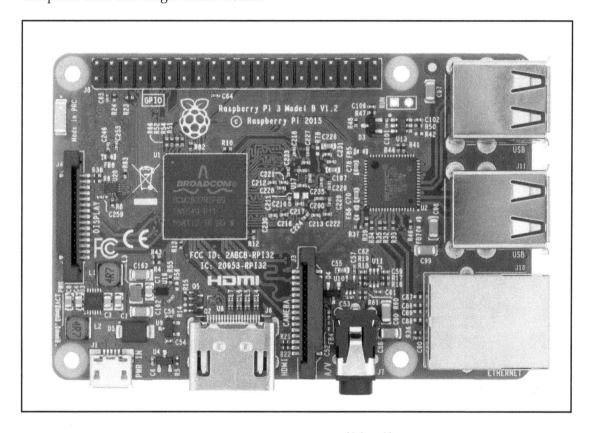

Figure 28: A Raspberry Pi, Model 3B; source: www.wikipedia.com

Equivalent to the size of a credit card, this single board computer offers the following:

- 1GB RAM
- 4 USB ports
- 40 GPIO pins
- A full HDMI port

- An Ethernet port
- Combined 3.5mm audio jack and composite video
- A Camera interface (CSI)
- A Display interface (DSI)
- A micro SD card slot
- A VideoCore IV 3D graphics core
- A 1.2GHz 64-bit quad-core ARMv8 CPU
- An 802.11n Wireless LAN
- Bluetooth 4.1
- Bluetooth Low Energy (BLE)

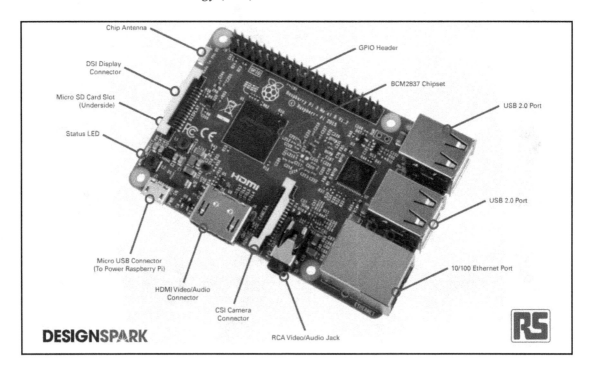

Figure 29: Raspberry Pi, Model 3b, layout details; source: www.smarthomesage.com

For less than 40 euros (which is the approximate cost of this board), for starters, you can simply connect a USB 2.0 mouse and keyboard to the USB ports, hook up a monitor via the HDMI port, and you already have the hardware setup of a personal computer:

Parameters	Description
SoC	Broadcom BCM2837
CPU	4x ARM Cortex-A53, 1.2GHz
GPU	Broadcom VideoCore IV
RAM	1GB LPDDR2
Networking	10/100 Ethernet, 2.4GHz 802.11n wireless
Bluetooth	Bluetooth 4 Classic, Bluetooth Low Energy
Storage	MicroSD
GPIO	40-pin header, populated
Ports	HDMI, 3.5mm analogue audio-video jack, 4xUSB, 2.0 Ethernet, Camera Serial Interface (CSI), Display Serial Interface (DSI)

Figure 30: Raspberry Pi, Model 3b, Specifications; source: www.smarthomesage.com

If you compare the specs of Raspberry Pi to a traditional desktop or laptop, you will find it somewhat lacking in many aspects, which it makes up for through its compact design and its purpose for existence, which is to be a low-cost computing device designed to promote teaching the intricacies of computers in schools and developing countries. Having used this device, I have come to believe in this design policy so much that in fact, on a personal note, I would have really loved to have Raspberry Pi as my first computer rather than the Intel Celeron Desktop System with 20 GB of hard disk and 128 MB of RAM, which I received on my 15th birthday (after burning a hole in my parents' pocket).

 Note that if you buy or order a Raspberry Pi board, then the accessories, that is, power supply, keyboard, monitor, mouse, and so on are not included by default. All that is included in the purchase is just the Raspberry Pi board itself. You still need to purchase the accessories (a power supply at the minimum) separately, which are essential to get you started.

After being initially introduced in February 2012 by the Raspberry Pi Foundation, this little computer has found its way to the desks of children, novices, and hackers alike. It has been used to create tablets, retro gaming systems, low cost desktop PCs and can even be found in drone and robotics applications:

Figure 31: A Raspberry Pi 7 tablet; source: learn.adafruit.com

So much for the hardware; what about the software for Raspberry Pi? Since an operating system is an integral part of any computer, Raspberry Pi can be a host to any of the many operating systems such as the following:

- Raspbian
- CentOS
- Fedora
- Ubuntu MATE
- Kali Linux
- Ubuntu Core
- Windows 10 IoT Core[1]
- RISC OS
- Slackware

- Debian
- Arch Linux ARM
- Android Things
- SUSE
- FreeBSD
- NetBSD

Out of these, one of the popular ones is Raspbian, which is a Debian-based operating system optimized for Raspberry Pi.

> For a detailed list of operating systems, which can run on Raspberry Pi hardware, visit `https://raspberrypi.stackexchange.com/questions/534/definitive-list-of-operating-systems`.

For first time users, installation can be quite a challenge; hence, to glide through it, **New Out Of Box Software** (**NOOBS**) is available, which is an easy operating system manager for Raspberry Pi.

> For information related to NOOBS and its setup, visit `https://www.raspberrypi.org/help/noobs-setup/2/`.

So, that's it, for the introduction to Raspberry Pi and now you are familiar with it, we will be setting this little computer up as a Beacon in Chapter 5, *Beacons with Raspberry Pi*.

Introduction to GitHub

To understand GitHub, you should first know what a Git is.

To explain what it is in simple terms, we should first understand how the actual software is crafted. It is carried out by multiple engineers working together in a team, often on the same source code files. When the software is being crafted, it often happens that within the development cycle, requirements might get changed or some of the features of the software might not even be required at all by the time of final release.

Perhaps an actual dialog between a product owner and a technical team lead might help you understand this situation better:

Ben (Product Owner) – *Hey Jerry, remember that hourly alarms feature we added to our app, the management has decided to remove that from this release.*

Jerry (Lead Developer) – *Sure. What I am going to do is disable that for now and then make a final release tomorrow after our testing cycle is complete.*

Ben – *Sounds Good!*

The next day, unfortunately, Jerry falls Sick and is now unable to come to the office. In the meantime, management has decided to enable the hourly alarms feature again. The responsibility for seeing that this is enabled when the app gets released is assigned to Ben. Since Jerry is not in the office, Ben is going to talk to Tom, who is Jerry's teammate, about this.

Ben – *Hey Tom, looks like we will need to enable that hourly alarms feature again, which Jerry disabled yesterday. Can you see to it that it is enabled when the release is made?*

Tom (Jerry's teammate) – *Sure Ben. I will* **checkout** *the code and enable it.*

Did you notice the jargon here? Tom used the word *checkout*; any idea what Tom is saying here?

The situation is actually similar to what we were discussing earlier, that is, when teams work they work on the same source code files, that means all the code is hosted on a single repository (in simple terms, a server). When Jerry had to disable the alarms feature, he downloaded (*checkout/pull*) the code from that repository, made the changes and uploaded (*push*) the updated code back again. Today, when Jerry is sick, Tom will be *checking out* (downloading) the code and will be following the same process.

Each time someone pushes a new piece of code, the version of the code is incremented and the code is labeled with a new version. This way, it makes it easier to see what changes were done in which version and by whom. All the versions are maintained as an internal list and in the case of a disaster (maybe Tom ends up deleting some important piece of functionality), one of the older working versions of the code can be restored:

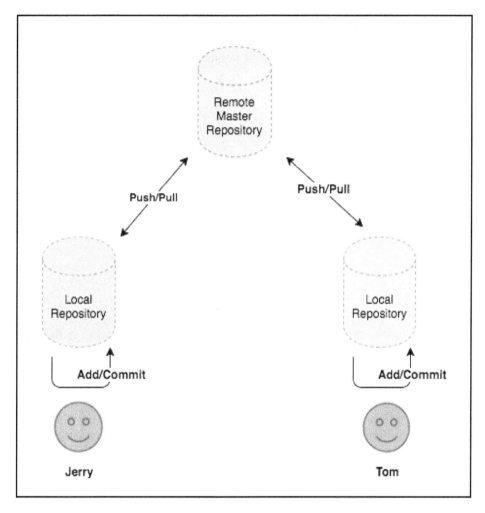

Figure 32: Version control system (Git) in action

This system that the team are using to manage their code is known as a **version control system**. There are many version control systems out there as follows:

- **Concurrent Versions System (CVS)**
- **Subversion (SVN)**
- **Git**
- **Mercurial**
- **Team Foundation Server (TFS)**

Git was designed and developed by one of the best hackers of our time, and the creator of Linux, Linus Torvalds. Over the course of this book, we will be using GitHub to store and download our code, which is just a web-based version of Git.

Started in February 2008, GitHub is currently the largest host of source code in the world.

 To register with and explore GitHub, visit `https://www.github.com`. The source code for various projects covered in this book will be available at `https://github.com/madhurbhargava`.

We would recommend registering and creating an account. This will provide you access to not only the source code for this book but also to a lot of other wonderful repositories of code written by Engineers at Google, Adobe, Twitter, PayPal, Dropbox, Facebook, and many others.

Summary

In this chapter, we've explored two of the most popular mobile operating systems, namely, Android and iOS, in a very hands-on manner by setting up development environments for both of them. We also went to our backend environment, Firebase, which allowed us to make the data from our Bluetooth Low Energy devices available to rest of the world. Not limiting ourselves to just software, we've learned about the Raspberry Pi, a very sophisticated piece of hardware, which we will later *magically* transform into a Bluetooth Low Energy beacon. Finally, we also learnt about GitHub, the world's largest host of source code, where we will be storing our code. We are all set up now and ready to take BLE knowledge to the next level.

Next up, to get an intuitive understanding of how Bluetooth Low Energy is implemented in wearables (for example, fitness trackers), with our recently gained knowledge about Sensors and Bluetooth Low Energy architecture, we will build an app that will help us look deep inside one of the popular Bluetooth Low Energy wearable/fitness tracking devices.

Building a Service Explorer App

3

I hear and I forget. I see and I remember. I do and I understand.

- Confucius

In the last chapter, we configured our systems so that we could build apps to gain a better understanding of Bluetooth Low Energy. In this chapter, we will build a Service Explorer app using which you can explore all kinds of Bluetooth Low Energy devices for their services. Also, as a bonus, we will simulate our very own homemade fitness tracker and explore its services and characteristics using the same app.

We hope that you remember our discussions regarding Bluetooth Low Energy architecture from the first chapter. Even if our deep discussions in the last chapter regarding the setup of our development environment has made it a little foggy, worry not, as we start with a refresher of the BLE architecture concepts in this chapter.

We will be creating a Service Explorer App by covering the following topics in this chapter:

- Central Peripheral Architecture for BLE
- Services and Characteristics
- Creating a Service Explorer App

Central Peripheral Architecture for BLE

As understanding of Bluetooth Low Energy architecture in terms of **Central** and **Peripheral** roles is essential to understand how Bluetooth Low Energy devices advertise and connect to each other.

A **Central** is a device, which scans for Bluetooth devices to connect and utilize the information hosted by them. Usually, **Central** devices are richer in terms of resources such as computing power compared to the **Peripheral** devices. Specific to the use case that we will describe in this chapter, the role of a **Central** will be played by a mobile phone (Android/iOS):

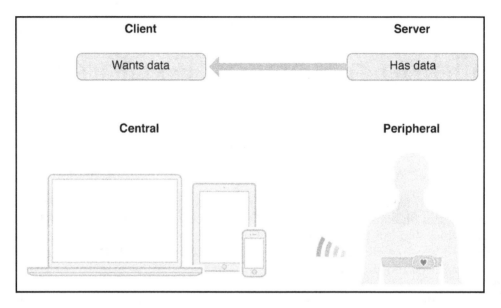

Figure 1: Central and Peripheral Roles in Bluetooth Low Energy; source: developer.apple.com

Peripherals, on the other hand, are devices, which advertise their presence, and it is by virtue of this advertisement that the **Central** knows that a **Peripheral** device is nearby and it can connect to enquire about its data. For this chapter, we will be using the following to act as peripherals:

- A fitness tracker
- A mobile app, which will simulate a heart rate tracking device

You should not just limit yourself to these two devices. Once we have designed the app, we recommend that you use it with as many BLE Peripherals as you can lay your hands on.

If the Peripheral is responsible for advertisements, then the Central is responsible for the following:

- Initiating a connection
- Establishing a connection
- Retrieving information from the peripheral (Discover Services, Characteristics, Descriptors and finally read the data)
- Terminating a connection

These are shown in the following image:

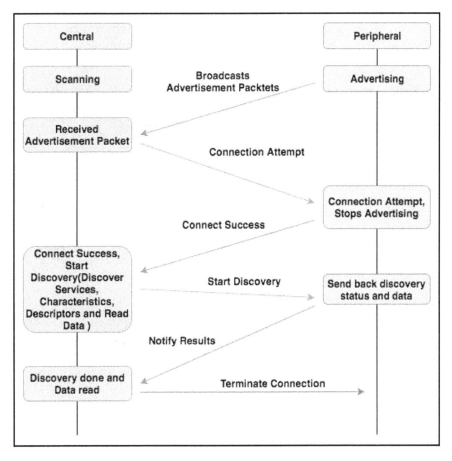

Fig 1.1 - Bluetooth Low Energy Connection Procedure

Based on the preceding points, it is safe to say that it is always the Central which is in control of the information exchange process and of the entire connection. For a one-to-one connection, depending on whether it is connected to a Central or not, a Bluetooth Low Energy Peripheral can be in either one of the following two states:

- Advertising
- Connected

When the Peripheral is in an **Advertising** state, it broadcasts Bluetooth Low Energy advertising packets. Before delving into the details of advertising packets, it is important to understand what the general packet structure is that BLE follows.

Basic BLE packets can range from 80 bits to 376 bits in length, which include a 1-byte preamble, 4-byte access codes correlated with the RF channel number used, a PDU that can be between 2 to 39 bytes, and 3 bytes of CRC.

 PDU is short for **Protocol Data Unit,** the term used to describe data as it moves from one layer of the OSI model to another. In this reference, PDU is often used synonymously with a packet.

An advertising PDU for the advertising channel consists of the 16-bit PDU header and depending on the type of advertising, the device address, and up to 31 bytes of information:

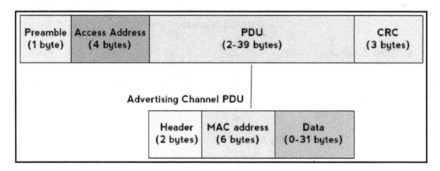

Figure 2: Over the air packet structure and advertisement PDU

However, although we have 31 bytes for packaging advertisement data, due to the specifications laid down by BLE, in reality, we have only 26 bytes. Puzzled? Let's see in the following points how it fits together:

- As per the Bluetooth Low Energy specifications, any GAP broadcast must contain flags that tell the device about the type of advertisement that is being sent. The structure of these flags uses three bytes in total: one for data length, one for data type, and one for the data itself. Hence, we have 28 bytes left.
- Now, finally we can package our own data but it also needs an indication of length and type (two bytes in total). So we have 26 bytes left to package the actual data.

Due to the Peripheral's advertisements, once a Central is aware of the existence of a Peripheral, in most cases, both Central and the Peripheral will intend to move towards the **Connected** state, primarily due to the fact that the Central will be interested in further exploring the data that the Peripheral has to offer.

 Opposing the preceding example are Beacons, which exist to advertise only and never try to move to a Connected state.

Once the connection has been made, a Central forms the process of discovery on the Peripheral, relying on the fact that the Peripheral has maintained its data in the form of services and their specific characteristics, as specified by the Bluetooth Low Energy specification.

Services and Characteristics

We have already covered services and characteristics in extensive detail in the first chapter; however, we will still do a quick refresher here, just in case. We will go bottom up this time starting with characteristics first.

Characteristics are the lowest and the most important echelon of the Bluetooth Low Energy technology. Encapsulated by a related service, these are the actual state variables, each of which stores a single piece of relevant measurement and information data. It is worthwhile reading about the Heart Rate Measurement characteristic, which we will be covering extensively in this chapter.

To read about the Heart Rate Measurement characteristic, visit `https://www.bluetooth.com/specifications/gatt/viewer?attributeXmlFile=org.bluetooth.characteristic.heart_rate_measurement.xml`.

Characteristics have a UUID, which can be 16-bit or 128-bit based on whether a characteristic has a standard or custom definition. A manufacturer is free to define custom characteristics, which are unique only to the manufacturer's software. However, to facilitate maximum interoperability between Bluetooth Low Energy devices it is always better to follow the definition of standard characteristics; a lot of devices still define custom characteristics due to security and privacy reasons. Bluetooth SIG defines a list of standard Bluetooth Low Energy characteristics here.

 To get a list of standard Bluetooth Low Energy characteristics, visit `https://www.bluetooth.com/specifications/gatt/characteristics`.

A service is a wrapper on top of data encapsulated in the characteristics. Similar kinds of data or characteristics are bundled together in a single service. This is a key factor in understanding the design of services, which exist to bundle similar kinds of data together. Perhaps a couple of examples will provide further clarity on this:

- Heart rate service: This consists of Heart Rate Measurement characteristic, sensor placement characteristic, and energy expanded characteristic
- Device information service: This consists of manufacturer name, model number, serial number, and hardware revision characteristics

Each service wraps similar or correlated data. For instance, if you want to get the Heart Rate Measurement data, then you should interrogate the heart rate service and if you need information about the device itself then you should interrogate the device service. The device service knows nothing about Heart Rate Measurement and the heart rate service is oblivious of the device manufacturer's name.

Like Bluetooth profiles, the Bluetooth SIG defines a number of official Services.

 You can visit `https://www.bluetooth.com/specifications/gatt/services` for more insight on service definitions by bluetooth SIG.

Each official service is assigned a unique 16-bit UUID so that it can distinguish itself from others; for example, a Heart Rate Service has a UUID of 0x180D. You can also write your own custom service for a specific purpose, but then it will need to have a 128-bit custom UUID.

Creating a Service Explorer App

The best way to test and master the theoretical knowledge is by doing and creating stuff and we will do the same by sticking to this well known and practiced philosophy. In this section, we will create a Service Explorer app for both Android and iOS platforms, which will help us in understanding the very intricacies of Bluetooth Low Energy as a technology. While similar in their functionalities, the Android app will scan manually through the use of start/stop buttons. The iOS app, however, will scan automatically as soon as the App is launched.

Following are the pre-requisites for this section,

Android:

- Latest Android Studio
- A Latest Android Device (Preferable Samsung Galaxy S8, since it has support for Bluetooth 5; otherwise Any Device with an API Level of 23(Android M) is fine)
- Basic familiarity with Java and Android

iOS:

- XCode 8.2
- A latest iOS device (Our development device uses iOS 9.3.5)
- Basic familiarity with Swift 2.3 and iOS

We request you to please do the following steps on a Mac based environment since then it would be possible to execute the steps for both Android and iOS on a single development environment.

Android

We begin by creating an empty project in the Android Studio. We have already done this exercise in the last chapter, so we will not be covering it here again.

While creating the Android Project, please choose the Minimum Api Level(minsdkversion) to be 23 since it supports all the Api calls that we would be using in this section.

Once we have finished creating our empty project (we have chosen the name of **AndroidBLEServiceExplorer** for our project with a package name of **packt.com.androidbleserviceexplorer** as shown below), as a first step, we can define some simple user interface, which will keep us informed of what is going on:

1. Configuring the UI: We will start by configuring the UI via the following steps. User interfaces in Android are primarily defined in xml files. If you have followed the project creation process exactly as defined in the last chapter, then, under the `layout` folder, there should be an `activity_main.xml` file as shown in the following screenshot(the code in the file might be different depending on the version of Android Studio. However, this should be of little concern since we are going to remove the code present in this file anyways):

Figure 3: Activity UI XML

2. We will create a really simple layout to see the results and begin by stripping the code in `activity_main.xml` file. Firstly, add `RelativeLayout` as a root element of your UI:

```xml
<RelativeLayout
 xmlns:android=
 "http://schemas.android.com/apk/res/android"
 xmlns:tools="http://schemas.android.com/tools"
 android:layout_width="match_parent"
 android:layout_height="match_parent"
 android:paddingBottom=
      "@dimen/activity_vertical_margin"
 android:paddingLeft="@dimen/activity_horizontal_margin"
 android:paddingRight="@dimen/activity_horizontal_margin"
 android:paddingTop="@dimen/activity_vertical_margin"
 tools:context=
 "packt.com.androidbleserviceexplorer.
  MainActivity">
</RelativeLayout>
```

A thorough understanding of Android's `RelativeLayout` is not necessary for this exercise, as there are plenty of resources out there which can help you in understanding the internals of `RelativeLayout`, the most popular being the Android developer website:`https://developer.android.com/guide/topics/ui/layout/relative.html`.

An important thing to keep in consideration while implementing the code mentioned above, the following line `tools:context="packt.com.androidbleserviceexplorer.MainActivity"` may throw an error if you directly copy the code as shown above and if your Project's package name is NOT `packt.com.androidservicebleexplorer`. Hence, please use the appropriate Package name in the aforementioned line.

3. To add to our interface design, we will be creating two buttons to give us the ability to stop and start the scanning process. Now, we add two buttons to `RelativeLayout` by adding the following two elements as direct children(inside the `RelativeLayout` Tag) to the parent `RelativeLayout`:

```xml
<Button android:layout_width="100dp"
android:layout_height="50dp"
android:text="Scan"
android:id="@+id/StartScanButton"
android:layout_marginTop="40dp"
android:layout_alignParentBottom="true"/>
```

```
<Button android:layout_width="wrap_content"
android:layout_height="50dp"
android:text="Stop Scanning"
android:id="@+id/StopScanButton"
android:layout_marginTop="40dp"
android:layout_alignParentBottom="true"
android:layout_alignRight=
"@+id/StartScanButton"/>
```

4. Next, we will also need to see what devices were found and, hence, we will also add the code for a ListView, just below the code for Buttons:

```
<ListView
android:layout_alignParentTop="true"
android:layout_width="match_parent"
android:layout_height="wrap_content"
android:layout_above="@+id/StartScanButton"
android:id="@+id/deviceListView"
android:stackFromBottom="false"/>
```

Although we are adding the ListView below the buttons in the code, it will still appear above the buttons due to its placement instructions, which we provide in this line: android:layout_above="@+id/StartScanButton".

5. **Configuring the App Permissions:** Since our UI is ready, we will now move on to configuring app permissions in the AndroidManifest.xml file.

On the Android operating system, each application runs in its own sandbox. If apps need to use any system or otherwise critical functions, then they need to explicitly request these permissions from the Android System via user intervention. The user can decide to grant these permissions or otherwise.

6. We will need the permissions related to Bluetooth and Location for our app. Locate the `AndroidManifest.xml` file(which can be found under under the manifests folder located in the root/near the top of the Project) in the project explorer. Add the following lines to the `AndroidManifest.xml` directly inside the `<manifest>` tag:

```
<uses-permission    android:name="android.permission.BLUETOOTH" />
<uses-permission android:name="android.permission.BLUETOOTH_ADMIN"
/>
<uses-permission    android:name=
"android.permission.ACCESS_COARSE_LOCATION" />
<uses-permission    android:name=
"android.permission.ACCESS_FINE_LOCATION" />
```

You must be wondering why the location permission is needed, the reason being that, Bluetooth Low Energy beacons can be used to get location information using BLE broadcast UUID data and an internet connection (for example, iBeacon and AltBeacon). Since this is possible and the data can be acquired via scan, a permission for location is required.

 To read more about permissions related to Bluetooth Low Energy on the Android platform, please visit: `https://developer.android.com/guide/topics/connectivity/bluetooth-le.html#setup`

Application Code

We have already created some UI and provided necessary permissions to our app, now we will add the necessary code to discover BLE services on any device. As the first step in this endeavour, it is important to discover the devices and then go over to the next step, which would be to discover the service on the device we are interested in.

Firstly, to control our UI elements (two `Button` and a `ListView`), we will need to access them in code:

1. Declare the following variables in the `MainActivity` class at the top in the `MainActivity.java` file:

```
Button startScanningButton;
Button stopScanningButton;
ListView deviceListView;
```

The `ListViews` in Android are backed by adapters, which hold the data being displayed in a `ListView`.

2. Also, declare an adapter and a device list to hold the data to be displayed in ListView:

```
ArrayAdapter<String> listAdapter;
ArrayList<BluetoothDevice> deviceList;
```

3. Once we have declared the necessary member variables, it is time to initialize them. Ideally, these variables should be initialized before the UI gets rendered on the screen; hence, please add the initialization code for each of these variables in the onCreate method of activity:

```
deviceListView = (ListView)
findViewById(R.id.deviceListView);
startScanningButton = (Button)
findViewById(R.id.StartScanButton);
stopScanningButton = (Button)
findViewById(R.id.StopScanButton);
stopScanningButton.setVisibility(View.INVISIBLE);
```

These lines will initialize the UI elements we introduced in the previous step and, after this, you can easily access them from your code. Failing to do this will only return a null pointer exception since in that case, you will be trying to use a member variable which has not been initialized. Also, notice that, in the last line, we make stopScanningButton invisible, which is due to the fact that we don't need the button initially (we only need it once we start scanning).

 To read more about the role of the onCreate method in the activity life cycle visit https://developer.android.com/reference/android/app/Activity.html.

4. Also, please initialize the adapters and the ArrayList we introduced in the previous step and set the same on ListView:

```
listAdapter = new ArrayAdapter<>
(this,android.R.layout.simple_list_item_1);
deviceList = new ArrayList<>();
deviceListView.setAdapter(listAdapter);
```

5. Also, we will need to add button click listeners to two of our buttons. For now, add two empty methods `startScanning()` and `stopScanning()` to the `MainActivity` class and initialize them as follows:

```
startScanningButton.setOnClickListener(new View.OnClickListener() {
public void onClick(View v) { startScanning(); } });
stopScanningButton.setOnClickListener(new   View.OnClickListener()
{ public void onClick(View v) { stopScanning(); } });
```

All of the preceding code is still happening inside the `onCreate` method and precisely in the order we are describing it.

Our UI initialization is done and is ready to interact via code. Now we will go ahead and declare BLE related member variables, which will help us to interact with Bluetooth stack and the Bluetooth Low Energy hardware on the Android device. I request that you pay close attention from here onwards because this is what the real core of our app will be.

6. We start by declaring three member variables in the `MainActivity` class to manage our Bluetooth Low Energy functionality:

```
BluetoothManager bluetoothManager;
BluetoothAdapter bluetoothAdapter;
BluetoothLeScanner bluetoothLeScanner;
```

The `BluetoothManager` is an instance of Bluetooth service running on Android devices and will help us in obtaining the instance of `bluetoothAdapter`.

To read more about `BluetoothManager`, visit `https://developer.android.com/reference/android/bluetooth/BluetoothManager.html`.

The `bluetoothAdapter` is the in-code representation of the actual Bluetooth Adapter present on the Android device.

To read more about `BluetoothAdapter`, visit `https://developer.android.com/reference/android/bluetooth/BluetoothAdapter.html`.

The `bluetoothLeScanner` has a descriptive name and true to its name, this class helps in scanning Bluetooth Low Energy Devices.

 To read more about `BluetoothLEScanner`, visit `https://developer.` `android.com/reference/android/bluetooth/le/BluetoothLeScanner.` `html`.

7. After declaring these Bluetooth Low Energy related member variables, we can initialize them like this in the `initialiseBluetooth` function and add the function call in `onCreate` method.

```
private void initialiseBluetooth() {
 bluetoothManager =
 (BluetoothManager) getSystemService
 (Context.BLUETOOTH_SERVICE);
bluetoothAdapter = bluetoothManager.getAdapter();
bluetoothLeScanner = bluetoothAdapter.getBluetoothLeScanner();
 }
```

Remember those two empty functions `startScanning` and `stopScanning`, that we added in Step 5, while initializing our UI. We will now add definitions for these functions.

8. Since we have the member variables for interacting with Bluetooth Low Energy functionality initialized, add the following definition to these functions to give the aforementioned methods a body:

```
public void startScanning() {
listAdapter.clear();
deviceList.clear();
 startScanningButton.setVisibility(View.INVISIBLE);
stopScanningButton.setVisibility(View.VISIBLE);
AsyncTask.execute(new Runnable() { @Override public void run() {
bluetoothLeScanner.startScan(leScanCallback); } });
 }

public void stopScanning() {
 startScanningButton.setVisibility(View.VISIBLE);
 stopScanningButton.setVisibility(View.INVISIBLE);
AsyncTask.execute(new Runnable() { @Override   public void run() {
bluetoothLeScanner.stopScan(leScanCallback); } });
 }
```

The startScanning() function clears our device list and list adapter, toggles the visibility of start and stop scanning buttons, and instructs the BluetoothLEScanner to start scanning. The stopScanning() function does exactly the opposite.

9. The BluetoothLEScanner requires a callback function(defined as leScanCallback below), which would be called for every device found and the devices found would be delivered as a result to this callback which we will define as follows:

```
// Device scan callback.
private ScanCallback leScanCallback = new ScanCallback() {
 @Override
 public void onScanResult(int callbackType, ScanResult result)
 {
   if (result.getDevice() != null) {
    if (!isDuplicate(result.getDevice())) {
     synchronized(result.getDevice()) {
      String itemDetail = result.getDevice().getName() == null ?
result.getDevice().getAddress() :
       result.getDevice().getName();
      listAdapter.add(itemDetail);
      deviceList.add(result.getDevice());
     }
    }
   }
  }
};
```

10. Inside the ScanCallback, onScanResult would be called for each device discovered and in our custom implementation of this method, we filter out the duplicates and append the filter results to the list. The filtering logic is in the isDuplicate() method:

```
private boolean isDuplicate(BluetoothDevice device){
for(int i = 0; i < listAdapter.getCount(); i++) {
String addedDeviceDetail =    listAdapter.getItem(i);
        if(addedDeviceDetail.equals(device.getAddress()) ||
addedDeviceDetail.equals(device.getName()))
{ return    true; } } return false;
}
```

11. Once we have a list of devices, we should be able to connect to a device and explore its services and characteristics. For this functionality, we will add a list item click listener on to each of our list items in the `onCreate` method as shown next, so that we can connect to the device and explore its services when the list item corresponding to that device is clicked:

```
deviceListView.setOnItemClickListener(new
AdapterView.OnItemClickListener() {
@Override public void onItemClick(AdapterView<?> parent, View view,
int position, long id) {
stopScanning();
listAdapter.clear();
BluetoothDevice device = deviceList.get(position);
device.connectGatt(MainActivity.this, true,
gattCallback); }
});
```

The `Listener` listens for the click on the item on the list and once the click happens, it stops scanning, cleans the list, and makes and connects to the device represented by that list item.

12. The `connectGatt` method requires a `BluetoothGattCallback`, where the results of connection state changes and service discovery would be delivered asynchronously. This can be defined as follows:

```
protected BluetoothGattCallback gattCallback = new
BluetoothGattCallback() {
@Override public void   onConnectionStateChange(BluetoothGatt
gatt, int status,   int newState) {
super.onConnectionStateChange(gatt, status, newState);
if (newState == BluetoothGatt.STATE_CONNECTED)  {
Log.i(TAG, "onConnectionStateChange() -  STATE_CONNECTED");
boolean discoverServicesOk = gatt.discoverServices();
} else if (newState ==   BluetoothGatt.STATE_DISCONNECTED) {
Log.i(TAG, "onConnectionStateChange() -  STATE_DISCONNECTED");}}
};
```

13. The `gattCallback` receives the updates for connection state changes and once the device is connected, we can instruct it to discover Services on the device through the callback itself. However, we override the `onServicesDiscovered()` method to get a result of service discovery:

```
@Override
public void onServicesDiscovered(BluetoothGatt gatt, int
status) {
super.onServicesDiscovered(gatt, status);
final List < BluetoothGattService > services =
gatt.getServices();
runOnUiThread(new Runnable() {
@Override
public void run() {
for (int i = 0; i < services.size(); i++) {
BluetoothGattService service = services.get(i);
StringBuffer buffer = new
StringBuffer
(services.get(i).getUuid().toString());
List < BluetoothGattCharacteristic > characteristics =
service.getCharacteristics();
for (int j = 0; j < characteristics.size(); j++) {
buffer.append("\n");
buffer.append("Characteristic:" +
characteristics.get(j).getUuid().toString());
}
listAdapter.add(buffer.toString());}}});
}
```

As services are discovered, the results will be delivered in the preceding callback. Hence, in the preceding method, we take this opportunity to update our UI with the results of service discovery as well as the details of each characteristic included in every service.

14. We are almost done with our setup, except for two things, namely, usability and permissions. Let's tackle usability first. It might very well happen that, when the user starts our app, they have their Bluetooth turned off. In such a case, it would be nice to prompt them to turn it on, which is exactly why we will add this piece of code in the `onCreate` method:

```
if (bluetoothAdapter != null &&
!bluetoothAdapter.isEnabled()) {
Intent enableIntent = new
Intent(BluetoothAdapter.ACTION_REQUEST_ENABLE);
startActivityForResult(enableIntent,      REQUEST_ENABLE_BT);
}
```

Also, please define REQUEST_ENABLE_BT in the MainActivity class as shown below:

```
private final static int REQUEST_ENABLE_BT = 1;
```

We have already handled an important aspect related to usability in our app. The second thing is security. From Android M onwards, we need to declare location permissions in the manifest as well as a request at runtime, which is done using the following code:

15. Add it to the `onCreate` method.

```
if
(this.checkSelfPermission(Manifest.permission.ACCESS_COARSE_LOC
ATION) !=    PackageManager.PERMISSION_GRANTED) {
  final AlertDialog.Builder builder = new
  AlertDialog.Builder(this);
  builder.setTitle("This app needs location access");
  builder.setMessage("Please grant location access so   this
app can detect peripherals.");
  builder.setPositiveButton(android.R.string.ok, null);
  builder.show();
}
```

And, we are done.

If you face any compilation issues, please refer to the Sample Project for which the link is provided towards the end of this section.

It is time to run the app and see what happens.

We request you that please run the App on the real device. Using Android Studio, it is as simple as connecting an Android device via USB to your Computer and pressing the Run Button. If you face problems specific to running/launching the App, more help is available at- `https://developer.android.com/training/basics/firstapp/running-app.html`

As soon as you launch the app and if your Bluetooth is turned off, the app will ask you if it can turn the Bluetooth on:

Figure 4: App asking for permission to turn the Bluetooth on

Once you have allowed it, the second thing the app will point out is that it needs location access:

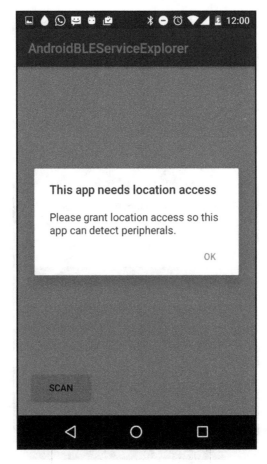

Figure 5: App pointing out that it needs location access

Following this dialog, you can exit the app or send it into the background, then enable **Location** on the device and also navigate to **Settings** | **Apps** | **Permissions** and enable the **Location** permission:

Figure 6: App Location permission in Settings

Once you have enabled **Location** and allowed location access, you can come back to the app and click on the **Scan** button:

Figure 7: Discovery results after pressing the Scan button

The app should display a list of Bluetooth Low Energy devices in the vicinity (if any). Our app is intelligent enough to display the name of each device; however, since the name is a user-configurable parameter for each BLE device and it might be possible that some devices do not have a name associated with them and in that case, it will display the MAC address of the devices. You can already see the Bluetooth Low Energy devices we found near our in the preceding figure.

Let's waste no more time and try to explore the Fitbit **Charge 2** device. On clicking the **Charge 2** item, the following result should be displayed (or at least our **Charge 2** displayed this at the time of this writing):

Figure 8: Results from the fitbit Charge 2 device

In the preceding figure, is a list of services found on the **Charge 2** device, and in the following figure each service is a list of the characteristics:

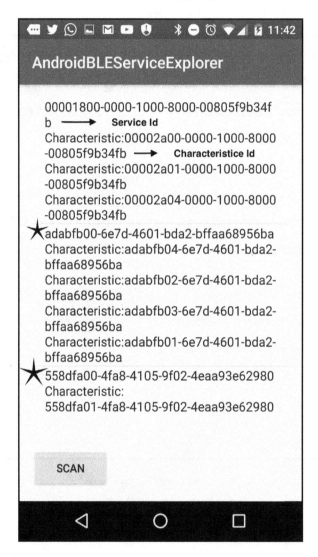

Figure 9: Services and their characteristics; custom services are marked by a star

Do you notice something that stands out?

There is no heart rate service (we know this since we do not see the Service ID 0x180D in the list of discovered services), which is interesting because fitbit advertises itself as a heart rate monitoring device, but there are no other standard services except a generic access service (0x1800) and a generic attribute service (0x1801). However, there are a couple of custom services (marked by stars in the preceding figure).

 To see the list of important services and IDs, visit `https://www.bluetooth.com/specifications/gatt/services`.

This brings us to an important conclusion and the fact which we also pointed out earlier. Although Bluetooth SIG provides you with specification and guidelines, it does not force you to follow these guidelines. Manufacturers are completely free to implement their custom services and characteristics. This is essential to understand since in real life you will come across many such devices, which advertise themselves as standard monitoring devices (heart rate, blood pressure, or weight monitors) but do not follow the standard specification, which is essentially due to the fact that they want to obfuscate their data from prying eyes, which fitbit is doing right now and, as responsible developers we should respect consumer security and privacy.

Henceforth, for the purpose of demonstration, we will *simulate* a perfect, *as per the specification* heart rate monitor. How will we do this? The popular answer is, *"There is an app for that"*, which will help us create our own homemade heart rate monitor.

To avoid breaking any laws and reading private data, we will use an already available app from the Google Play store, to create our own heart rate monitor. This app lets the hosting device simulate and behave as a BLE Peripheral. We will use this app to simulate a heart rate monitoring device. This way we are not breaching any privacy policies nor exposing any sensitive data. Henceforth, we will make use of two Android devices; one will be simulating as a heart rate monitor and the other will run our app to detect the heart rate reading being advertised. You can use your Android device to navigate to the link mentioned next, in order to download the BLE Peripheral Simulator app.

Navigate to the link from your Android device to install the BLE Peripheral Simulator `https://play.google.com/store/apps/details?id=io.github.webbluetoothcg.bletestperipheral`.

1. Once you have installed the BLE Peripheral Simulator, start the app after making sure you have turned on Bluetooth, the location on the device, and provided location permission of the app. The app should display a list of peripherals it can simulate:

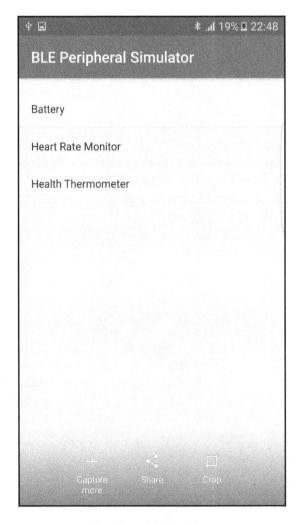

Figure 10: BLE Peripheral Simulator

2. Click on the list item that says **Heart Rate Monitor**. Once you are on the screen shown in the following screenshot, that means the Android device on which the Peripheral Simulator is running, is now advertising (until the screen is on) as a **Heart Rate Monitor**. Let's try searching this peripheral via our app:

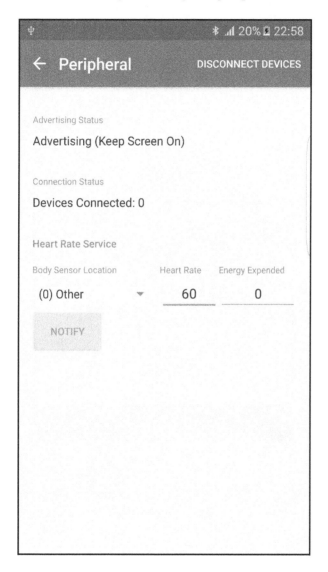

Figure 11: Heart Rate Monitor Simulator Advertising and Settings Screen

3. Let's start our app and try searching the BLE Peripheral Simulator:

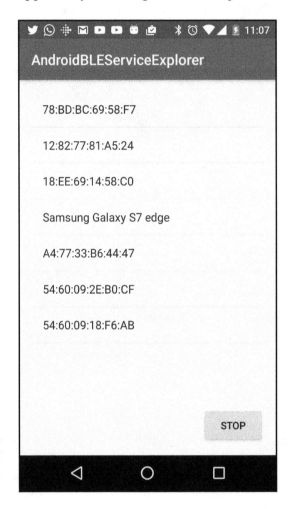

Figure 12: Discovering the BLE Peripheral Simulator

I am running the BLE Peripheral Simulator on a Samsung Galaxy S7 Edge device; as you can see in the preceding figure, we can see it as the advertising device.

The Peripheral app advertises with the Bluetooth name of the device it is being hosted on.

4. Let's connect to the device by clicking on the **List** item, which says Samsung Galaxy S7 edge (in your case, it will depend on the device you are using) and see if we can find our precious Heart Rate Service:

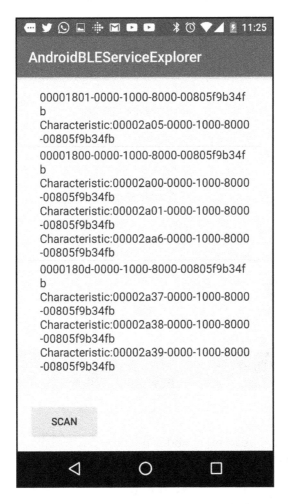

Figure 13: Services on the simulated Heart Rate BLE Peripheral Monitor

And, if you notice, as per the specification, right at the bottom is the **Heart Rate Service**, starting with the UUID of 0x180d.

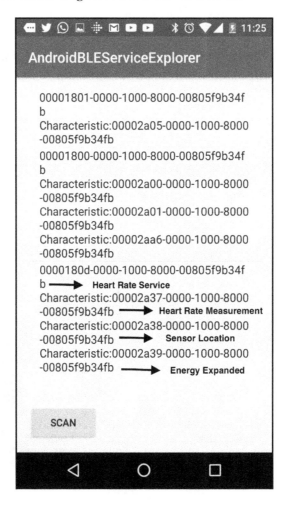

Figure 14: Heart Rate Service and its Characteristics

You can read more about how the data is structured in a **Heart Rate Service** in the link mentioned next.

To read more about the **Heart Rate Service**, visit `https://www.bluetooth.com/specifications/gatt/viewer?attributeXmlFile=org.bluetooth.service.heart_rate.xml`.

5. Now we can update our existing app to read the Heart Rate Measurement characteristic and upload it to the Firebase Cloud. Add the following two IDs to a list of member variables of the MainActivity class:

```
private final String HEART_RATE_SERVICE_ID = "180d";
public final String HEART_RATE_MEASUREMENT_ID = "2a37";
```

These will help us in identifying the Heart Rate Service and which characteristic should be read for the Heart Rate measurement. These IDs are as per the Bluetooth SIG Specification and to understand that how and why are we using these. You can read more about the Heart Rate Service at the link mentioned next.

To read more about Heart Rate Service, its characteristics, and associated IDs, visit https://www.bluetooth.com/specifications/gatt/viewer? attributeXmlFile=org.bluetooth.service.heart_rate.xml.

6. Now we need to read the Heart Rate measurement characteristic from the Heart Rate Service. A good place to do so would be the service discovery process or the onServicesDiscovered method, which we have already over-ridden. Add the following piece of code:

```
if  (buffer.toString().contains(HEART_RATE_SERVICE_ID)) {
if(characteristics.get(j).getUuid().toString().contains(HEART_R
ATE_MEASUREMENT_ID)
{gatt.setCharacteristicNotification(characteristics.get(j),
true);}
}
```

The preceding code needs to be added just after the following line in the onServicesDiscovered method:

```
buffer.append("Characteristic:"+characteristics.get(j).getU
uid().toString());
```

The preceding code enables notifications for the Heart Rate Measurement value and our app will receive a value update whenever you press the **NOTIFY** button on the BLE Peripheral Simulator app:

Figure 15: Notify Button on BLE Peripheral Simulator App

We have added the code to enable Notifications for the Heart Rate measurement value, but how and where do we receive these Notifications? We address this final missing piece in the next step.

7. Just as in the case of onServicesDiscovered method, which the Android BLE framework calls as soon as it discovers Services on a BLE Peripheral, there is another callback which happens whenever notification on a particular characteristic occurs. In our case, we have enabled notifications on the Heart Rate Measurement characteristic and we need to override the method mentioned in the following code to be notified for the values related to the characteristic:

```
public void onCharacteristicChanged(BluetoothGatt gatt,
BluetoothGattCharacteristic characteristic) {
  if
  (characteristic.getUuid().toString().
   contains(HEART_RATE_MEASUREMENT_ID)) {
  int flag = characteristic.getProperties();
  int format = -1;
  if ((flag & 0x01) != 0) {
  format =        BluetoothGattCharacteristic.FORMAT_UINT16;
  } else {
  format = BluetoothGattCharacteristic.FORMAT_UINT8;
  }
  final int heartRate =        characteristic.getIntValue(format,
  1);
  Log.d(TAG, String.format("Received heart rate: %d", heartRate));
  }
  }
```

This will extract the value of the Heart Rate Measurement from the characteristic as soon as the notification related to the characteristic is received.

 To understand how data is structured in a Heart Rate Measurement characteristic, visit https://www.bluetooth.com/specifications/gatt/ viewer?attributeXmlFile=org.bluetooth.characteristic.heart_rate_ measurement.xml.

Now, if you run the app | Discover the BLE Peripheral Simulator | Connect to the Simulated Heart rate monitor, then our app should enable notifications on the Heart Rate Measurement characteristics as soon as it discovers it and if you press the **Notify** button on the BLE Peripheral Simulator, then you should see the following statement in the Android Studio logs:

```
packt.com.androidbleserviceexplorer D/BLEPackt: Received heart rate: 60
```

The statement should repeatedly occur as many times as you press the **Notify** button on the BLE Peripheral Simulator.

We now have the data, and all that remains is to upload it to a server so that it can be remotely accessible to anyone who wants to read/access it. For this, we will integrate Firebase into our Android app and upload the same measurement that we received to the Firebase Cloud.

1. To integrate Firebase, in the Android Studio, on the top **Menu** bar, navigate to **Tools | Firebase**. This should bring up the Firebase **Assistant** window as shown in the following screenshot:

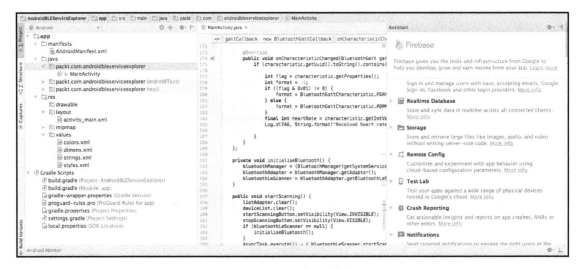

Figure 16: Firebase Assistant

2. Under the Firebase **Assistant** window, navigate to **Realtime Database | Save And Retrieve data**. This should bring up the save and retrieve data window.

3. Click on **Connect your app to Firebase** in this window. The Firebase connection should ask you then to choose an existing project or create a new one.

4. Choose to create a new one and click on **Connect to Firebase**:

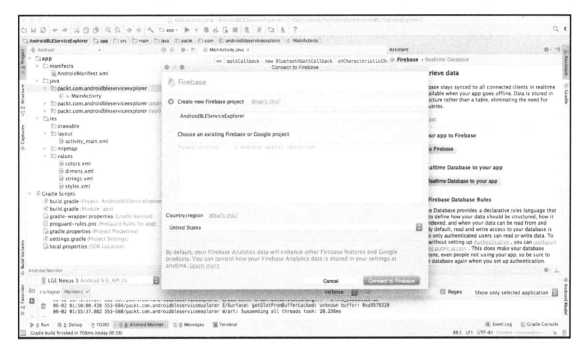

Figure 17: Creating a new Firebase Project

5. The process will take a few minutes and, on successful completion, the indicator below **Connect your app to Firebase** in the **Assistant** window will turn green.

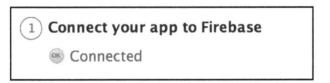

Figure 18: Firebase App connection status

6. Now, click on the second item in the **Assistant** window, which says **Add the Realtime Database to your app**. A prompt comes up which is essentially asking whether necessary changes regarding the inclusion of Firebase can be made to the project. Click on **Accept Changes** in this prompt:

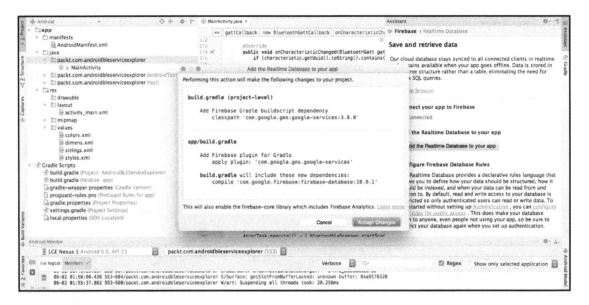

Figure 19: Adding Firebase to the project

7. After accepting the changes, a Gradle Sync will start.

8. Post the Gradle Sync, and click on **Configure your rules for public access** under step 3 in the assistant window. This step will open the browser with some Firebase documentation.

9. Click on **Go to Console** on the top-right corner of this screen. This should open up a dashboard/gallery of existing applications.

10. Choose the relevant application name; in our case it is
    AndroidBLEServiceExplorer:

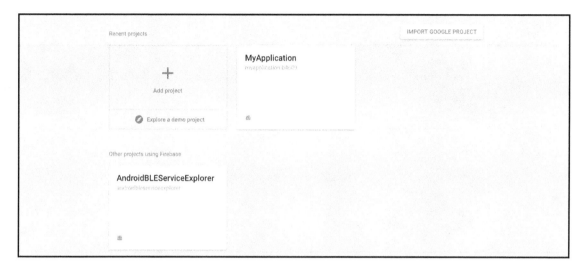

Figure 20: Firebase apps console

11. You should be taken to a detailed console. From here, click on **Database** in the
    left pane and select the **Rules** tab from the list of horizontal tabs.

12. What you should be seeing in front of you is a JSON file signifying rules as key-
    value pairs:

    1. Change the `.read` key from `auth != null` to `true`.
    2. Do the same for the `.write` key.
    3. Hit the **Publish** button on the top.

This configuration is for demo purposes only, which means anyone can read or write to your database. In the real world, your rules will be more advanced and sophisticated than this.

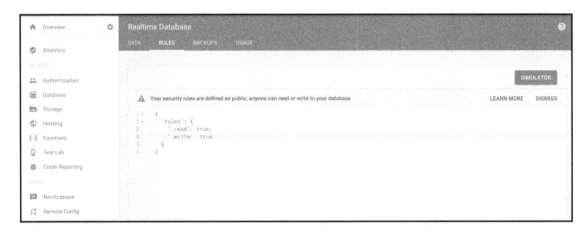

Figure 21: Firebase Detailed Console and Rules

13. Once you have made the changes, in our Android app, add the following code to send the data to the cloud:

```
// Write a message to the database
FirebaseDatabase database =      FirebaseDatabase.getInstance();
DatabaseReference myRef =  database.getReference("heartrate");
myRef.setValue(new Integer(heartRate).toString());
```

The preceding code needs to be added just below the following line in the `onCharacteristicChanged` method:

```
Log.d(TAG, String.format("Received heart rate: %d", heartRate));
```

14. Run our Android app | Discover Services on the BLE Heart Rate Monitor Peripheral Simulator.

15. Once Services have been discovered, click on the **Notify** button on the BLE Heart Rate Monitor Peripheral Simulator.

16. Navigate to the Firebase Console and Voila! Under the **Data** tab, you should see the value of Heart Rate Measurement getting updated on the console:

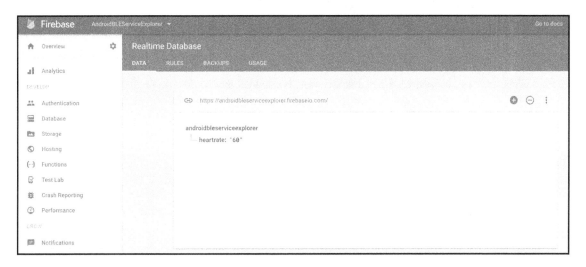

Figure 22: Heart Rate Value getting uploaded to Firebase Cloud

Now, this value is available for anyone who is interested, which could possibly be a caregiver or a healthcare provider.

So far, so good! You just finished an end to end Bluetooth Low Energy project on Android complete with backend integration. All the code from that which we went over in this section is available on the GitHub link mentioned next.

 For the Android BLE Service Explorer app code, visit `https://github.com/madhurbhargava/AndroidBLEServiceExplorer`.

Now we move to iOS, where we will jump start the BLE development and hit the ground running; however, we will also expect that you as a user would implement a small part of the functionality on your own.

On to iOS then!

iOS

For iOS, we begin in a similar manner as we did with Android: an empty project. We start by creating a Single View Application as described in `Chapter 2`, *Setting Up*, and name our app `iOSBLEServiceExplorer` and get started with project creation as described in the last chapter.

 To run on an actual device, you will need to create an Apple ID and generate a signing certificate associated with that ID. You can find the complete process at `http://blog.ionic.io/deploying-to-a-device-without-an-apple-developer-account/`.

To keep you focused on the core concepts, we will keep our iOS app as simple as possible:

1. We start by creating an empty project by the name of `iOSBLEServiceExplorer`. If the project creation was successful, then you should be presented with the project in Xcode as shown in the following screenshot:

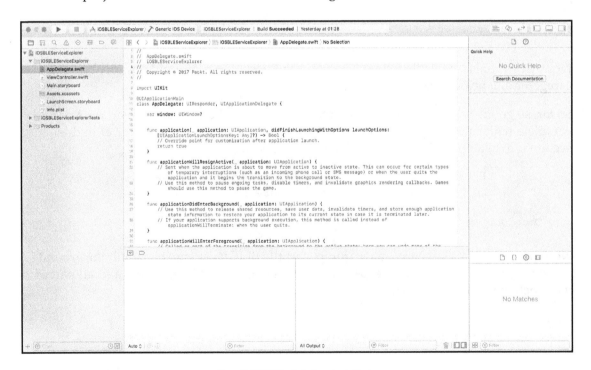

Figure 23: iOSBLEServiceExplorer App in Xcode

2. You should be presented with a list of files as shown in the Project Navigator, the major ones being, **ViewController.swift**, **Main.storyboard**, and **AppDelegate.swift**. We will mainly be interacting with the ViewController, for the logic, and the storyboard for the UI.

3. UI in iOS is primarily defined in storyboards and xib files. In our app, we will be using the storyboard. Navigate to the **Main.storyboard** file and drag and drop a TextView in the view area:

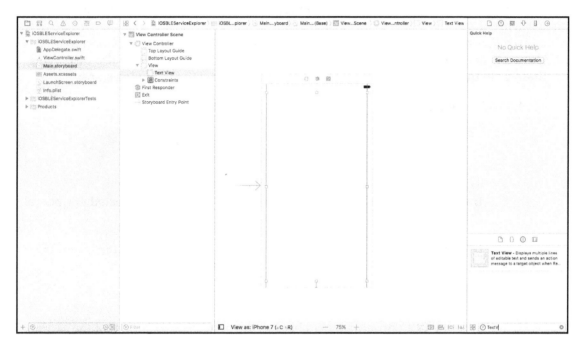

Figure 24: Storyboards for UI in iOS

Make it occupy the screen by giving it a small margin of 8 px from left, top, right, and bottom of the parent.

 To read more about margins and other layout constraints, visit `https://developer.apple.com/library/content/documentation/UserExperience/Conceptual/AutolayoutPG/WorkingwithConstraintsinInterfaceBuidler.html`.

4. Also create an IBOutlet from the TextView to the code, so that the view can be accessed from the code. Name the IBOutlet as *textView*.

To read more about IBOutlets and in general about connecting UI to code, visit `https://developer.apple.com/library/content/ referencelibrary/GettingStarted/DevelopiOSAppsSwift/ ConnectTheUIToCode.html`.

We are done with our UI. Now, let's define our logic for interacting with BLE devices.

We will take a slightly different approach this time as compared to Android while interacting with the nearby Bluetooth Low Energy devices via iOS. In Android, we used to display a list of devices found to the user and then let the user decide which device he/she wanted to explore in terms of services and characteristics. In iOS, we will connect to each device as it is discovered and explore its services and characteristics, while also displaying the findings to the user. Sounds like fun? Let's code this using the following steps:

1. Add a `CBCentralManager` member variable called manager to the `ViewController` class as follows:

   ```
   var manager:CBCentralManager!
   ```

   The `CBCentralManager` objects(provided by the `CoreBluetooth` framework in iOS) are used to manage discovered and connected peripheral (`CBPeripheral`) objects.

To read more about `CBCentralManager`, visit `https://developer.apple. com/reference/corebluetooth/cbcentralmanager`.

2. Initialize the CBCentralManager object in the *viewDidLoad* method of the ViewController as follows:

   ```
   override func viewDidLoad() { super.viewDidLoad()
   manager = CBCentralManager(delegate: self, queue: nil)
   }
   ```

Now, we need to start scanning for nearby devices. CBCentralManager has various methods which allow us to perform scanning and connecting to various devices. We can use the scanForPeripherals method to scan for nearby peripherals; however, the question remains as to what point of time should the scanning start. We can always start scanning at the click of a button; however, we would like to take this opportunity to introduce you to the CBCentralManagerDelegate protocol. CBCentralManager does all the heavy lifting for you; however, most of the Bluetooth tasks happen asynchronously (discovery and getting discovered devices). Hence, we need to adopt our view controller to this protocol as we need the results of the discovery process.

To read more about CBCentralManagerDelegate, visit https://developer.apple.com/reference/corebluetooth/cbcentralmanagerdelegate.

Consider the methods of this delegate similar to the callbacks(GattCallback) that we defined in our earlier Android Code.

3. Adapt the ViewController to the CBCentralManagerDelegate protocol as shown here:

```
class ViewController: UIViewController,
CBCentralManagerDelegate
```

4. Make the CBCentralManager object aware that the ViewController class is the delegate where it should deliver results of the discovery by adding the following code in viewDidLoad:

```
manager.delegate = self
```

5. The CBCentralManager object has a state and, as soon as you initialize it, its state gets updated. You can receive these state changes and updates in the centralManagerDidUpdateState method of CBCentralManagerDelegate.

To read more about states of CBCentralManager, visit https://developer.apple.com/reference/corebluetooth/cbcentralmanagerstate.

6. It is also a good idea to instruct the manager to start scanning for devices as soon as it is in `poweredOn` state. For this, you need to implement the `centralManagerDidUpdateState` method as shown in the following code:

```
func centralManagerDidUpdateState(_ central:   CBCentralManager) {
  if central.state == .poweredOn {
central.scanForPeripherals(withServices: nil,   options: nil) }
  else { print("Bluetooth not   available.") }
}
```

The first parameter of the `scanForPeripherals` method instructs the manager that it should only search for Peripherals with some specific services. When you pass `nil` for both the parameters, you are essentially instructing the manager to find all the advertising peripherals without any filtering.

 To read more about `CBCentralManager`, visit `https://developer.apple.com/reference/corebluetooth/cbcentralmanager`.

7. We initiated the scan in the previous step; now how do we get the results? Implement the method shown in the following code for this purpose:

```
public func centralManager(_ central: CBCentralManager, didDiscover
peripheral: CBPeripheral, advertisementData: [String : Any], rssi
RSSI: NSNumber)      {

let device = (advertisementData as NSDictionary) .object(forKey:
CBAdvertisementDataLocalNameKey) as? NSString

if device != nil {
textView.text.append("===Device Name:\(device) \n")
manager.connect(peripheral, options: nil)
}
}
```

The preceding method is from the CBCentralManagerDelegate class, which we adopted in step 3.

The CBCentralManager object will keep reporting the devices found to the preceding method. We will be displaying the device details and connecting to each device as and when it is discovered.

If the CBCentralManager object is able to connect to the device/peripheral successfully, then the following method will be called via the delegate:

```
        public func centralManager(_ central:   CBCentralManager,
    didConnect peripheral: CBPeripheral)    { peripheral.delegate = self
    peripheral.discoverServices(nil)  }
```

This is a good opportunity for us to initiate service discovery on the peripheral. As the name suggests, the discoverServices method initiates service discovery on the peripheral and, by passing in nil as a parameter, we are requesting it to apply no filtering at all and to discover and report all services as is. Also, just like the CBCentralManager object, the CBPeripheral object needs a delegate to report the results.

 To read more about CBPeripheral, visit https://developer.apple.com/reference/corebluetooth/cbperipheral.

Hence, we will adapt our ViewController class to the CBPeripheralDelegate object as shown here:

```
class ViewController: UIViewController, CBCentralManagerDelegate,
CBPeripheralDelegate
```

Now, our service class is adapted to both CBCentralManagerDelegate as well CBPeripheralDelegate or, in simple terms, it is going to receive updates for both actions taken by the central, as well as the peripheral.

 To read more about CBPeripheralDelegate, visit https://developer.apple.com/reference/corebluetooth/cbperipheraldelegate.

As and when the service discovery is done, the Peripheral will report its results to the delegate's method mentioned next:

```
public func peripheral(_ peripheral: CBPeripheral, didDiscoverServices
error: Error?) {
if let services = peripheral.services {
for service in services {

textView.text.append("Service found:\(service.uuid.uuidString) for device
\(peripheral.name) \n") textView.text.append("\n")

peripheral.discoverCharacteristics(nil, for: service) }
} }
```

Along with the device details of the device discovered, which we displayed on the screen previously, we now add details of each service. We also instruct the peripheral to discover all the characteristics for the service.

The characteristics will be reported to the following `delegate` method; hence, you need to add it to the `ViewController` class:

```
public func peripheral(_ peripheral: CBPeripheral,
didDiscoverCharacteristicsFor service: CBService, error: Error?) {
if let characteristics = service.characteristics {
for characteristic in characteristics {

textView.text.append("Characteristic
found:\(characteristic.uuid.uuidString) for
Service:\(service.uuid.uuidString) for device \(peripheral.name) \n")

textView.text.append("\n")

} } }
```

And, we are done. If you start and launch the app, then you should see detailed information, that is, device name, service included, and characteristics in each service, for each peripheral discovered by the Central:

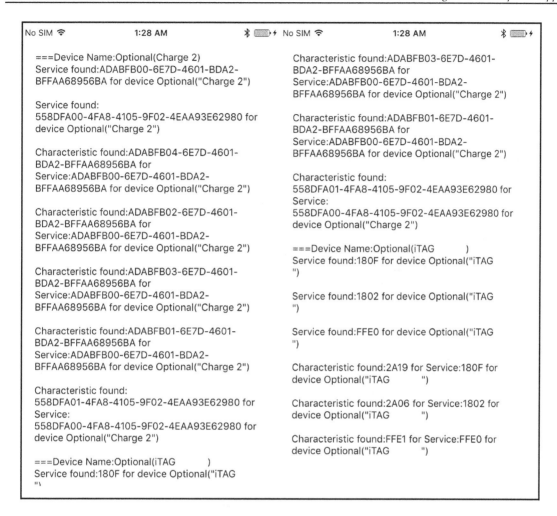

Figure 25: iOS BLE Service Explorer app on iOS

We have already done most of the heavy lifting in the preceding code by scanning, connecting, and service discovery for the iOS BLE Peripherals. All the code that we discussed in this section is available on the link mentioned next.

For the iOS BLE Service Explorer app code, visit `https://github.com/ madhurbhargava/iOSBLEServiceExplorer`.

We encourage the readers to attempt to configure notifications for characteristics on discovered services.

To read more about Core Bluetooth Framework on iOS, visit `https:// developer.apple.com/library/content/documentation/ NetworkingInternetWeb/Conceptual/CoreBluetooth_concepts/ AboutCoreBluetooth/Introduction.html`.

Remember, iOS may be a different platform to Android; however, the technology and the process remain the same; that is, **Scan | Connect | Discover Services | Discover Characteristics | Configure Indications/Notifications for Characteristics | Process the Data**.

Summary

If you covered this chapter completely and have made it this far, then you can give yourself a pat on the back. Having an understanding of Bluetooth Low Energy on two major mobile platforms is no small feat.

As your creative juices start flowing, you will have realized the endless possibilities that Bluetooth Low Energy can generate together when combined with a backend. For example, reading data from a heart rate monitor (or any other BLE Peripheral) is one thing, but making it available to be accessed remotely, already opens doors to many interesting IoT applications of Bluetooth Low Energy, which are not just limited to healthcare.

There is so much more to come and, in the coming chapters we will go in even deeper and explore how we can make use of Bluetooth Low Energy in areas other than healthcare, such as indoor positioning/navigation, Beacon based local adverts and other commercial solutions.

In the next chapter, we will shift our focus away a little bit from the healthcare and traditional discovery of services and characteristics for BLE. We will be focusing more on device advertisements, proximity, and how IoT plays a role together with Bluetooth Low Energy in personal tracking, by using this information.

4
Designing a Personal Tracking System

The usefulness of the cup is in its emptiness

- Bruce Lee

We have already covered the practical aspects of arranging data in profiles, services, and characteristics as part of Bluetooth Low Energy implementation in the peripheral devices in the `Chapter 3`, *Building a Service Explorer App.*

In this chapter, we take a break from these discussions and focus on another very interesting and lesser known aspect/parameter related to Bluetooth Low Energy, namely, **Received Signal Strength Indication (RSSI)**, which we will eventually use to detect the proximity/distance (yes, you read that right) to a Bluetooth Low Energy device.

Note that there are BLE devices already available, which support Find Me and Proximity BLE Profiles which can be used to accomplish this task in a very simple and similar manner (Scan|Detect and subscribe to notifications from the relevant characteristics) as we subscribed to heart rate notifications in the `Chapter 3`, *Building a Service Explorer App.* However, we would not like to repeat what has already been covered and, instead, we'll build something which is relatively new, very leading edge and still in experimental phases.

Hence, we will be relying on a lot of research papers to build a proximity-based personal tracker from the ground up (rather than relying on a Find Me or Proximity Profile based service on the iTag device), which we will be doing by covering the following topics in this chapter:

- RSSI and Proximity
- Indoor Proximity and Localization with an iTag
- Designing the Tracking App

Also, at the time of writing this chapter, Samsung Galaxy S8 had already hit the market shelves and luckily we were able to lay our hands on one. Henceforth, we would be executing all our code on the Bluetooth Low Energy 5 stack included in the Galaxy S8 mobile device.

RSSI and Proximity

In simplest terms, RSSI is the measure of strength of a radio signal in a wireless environment. It is the measured in **decibel milliwatts (dbm)**.

As a rule of thumb, the higher the RSSI, the stronger the signal. RSSI tells us whether the signal is getting stronger or weaker and we can use this fact to our advantage by approximating the proximity of the broadcasting Bluetooth Low Energy device.

Since you now understand what RSSI is, then, not going into too much detail, we can safely say that, if given a list of RSSI values, then just by looking at these values we can already guess whether the broadcasting BLE device is nearby or far away. We will elaborate on this fact through the following RSSI values:

-44, -51, -62, -60, -62

Figure 1: Typical RSSI values

Can you already guess what do these RSSI values mean?

> Don't worry if you do not understand how these RSSI values were generated; we will be covering that in detail when we design the tracking app.

Well, first things first: if you haven't already noticed, the preceding values are in a decreasing order and they were generated by gradually moving a broadcasting iTag away from a receiving Android device:

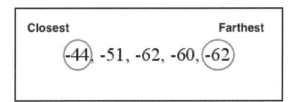

Figure 2: RSSI Value Details

Hence, **-44** was generated when the iTag was closest and **-62** was generated when the iTag was farthest away. Now the trick is to convert this RSSI into an accurate distance/proximity value, which actually tells us the distance between the broadcasting iTag and the receiving device.

Our task in this chapter would be, to design an algorithm as a part of an app, which runs on the receiving device, receives the RSSI from the iTag, and converts it to an accurate distance of the iTag from the receiver.

Another thing to notice in the preceding figure is that there is a **-60** surrounded by **-62**. It looks as if the iTag was being moved further and then moved closer again before being moved away finally. However, that is not the case; the **-60** value is there because RSSI tends to fluctuate a lot. Rather than being a fixed value, RSSI tends to fluctuate, mostly due to external factors influencing radio waves—such as absorption, interference, or diffraction:

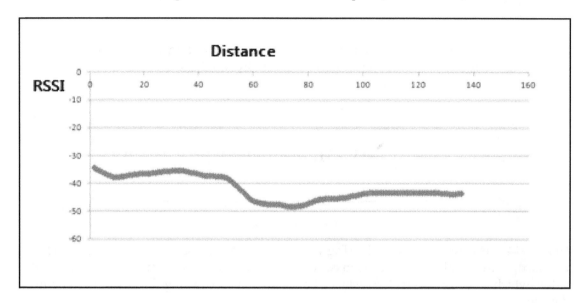

Figure 3: Rather than being a fixed value, RSSI is a trend; source: www.bluetooth.com

Since RSSI is a trend, our algorithm will have to rely on the most frequently occurring value from a sample of values.

Many researchers are already working on how to get more accurate indoor localization results based on RSSI, and we will be drawing on the findings of one such research project.

 To read and learn about the research related to the conversion of RSSI to distance, navigate to `http://s2is.org/Issues/v1/n2/papers/paper14. pdf`.

Our next step will be to identify the sensors we will be using for the task at hand.

Indoor Proximity and Localization with an iTag

With the advent of Bluetooth Low Energy, a technology which is rapidly maturing, it has already started to find its way into a variety of premises.

iTags are small Bluetooth Low Energy sensors, which can be planted on things or individuals (especially toddlers) to track whether the iTag is nearby or far away:

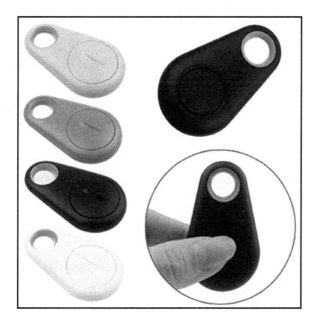

Figure 4: iTag; source: www.amazon.com

You can buy an iTag for a few Euros online or at a nearby electronics shop.

The Bluetooth implementation of an iTag usually consists of a Link Loss and Immediate Alert Service.

To read more about the Immediate Alert Service in detail, visit `https://www.bluetooth.com/specifications/gatt/viewer?attributeXmlFile=org.bluetooth.service.immediate_alert.xml`.

Apart from many other functionalities, the Immediate Alert and Link Loss services are used for providing alerts when the device link is lost.

To read more about the Link Loss Service in detail, visit `https://www.bluetooth.com/specifications/gatt/viewer?attributeXmlFile=org.bluetooth.service.link_loss.xml`.

iTags are usually coupled with an app, which interacts with these services and indicates its proximity. It causes alerts (via beeps or alarm sounds) when the device link is lost.

Instead of the traditional manner of interaction with a Bluetooth Low Energy Device via its services and characteristics, in this chapter, we interact with the iTag in a nontraditional way via reading the RSSI value from the iTag and approximating the proximity/distance of a mobile device from the iTag based on that.

An iTag might not be as accurate as most of the commercial beacon-based solutions out there; however, it is enough to build and demonstrate a solid proof of concept, which states that apart from interacting with just services and characteristics, Bluetooth Low Energy has a lot more to offer.

Designing the Tracking App

As already indicated, in this section, we will be designing an app for both Android and iOS platforms, which listens for RSSI updates from a broadcasting iTag sensor and uses these values to predict the distance of the iTag from the receiver.

Our development pre-requisites and setup remain exactly similar to those defined in `Chapter 3`, *Building a Service Explorer App*.

Android

We begin by creating an empty project in the Android Studio. We have chosen the name `AndroidiTagPersonalTracker`; feel free to be creative with your project's name. We have already done this exercise in `Chapter 2`, *Setting Up*; hence, we will not be covering that here again.

When you are creating any Android-based Bluetooth Low Energy Project, remember to select the minimum API Level as 21 during the setup, since many Bluetooth Low Energy related system API calls require minimum API level 21.

Once we have finished creating our empty project, as a first step, we can define some simple user interface, which will keep us informed about what is going on:

1. From the knowledge we gained in the previous chapter, we already know that, user interfaces in Android are primarily defined in xml files. If you followed the project creation process exactly as defined in the `Chapter 3`, *Building a Service Explorer App*, then under the layout folder there should be an **activity_main.xml** file as shown next. Also, if you notice, there is a slight difference here; in `Chapter 3`, *Building a Service Explorer App*, we based our Layout on Relative Layout, while in this chapter, for the purpose of introducing the newly and highly recommended way of designing a UI in Android, it will be based on a new `ViewGroup` introduced by Android, that is, `ConstraintLayout`:

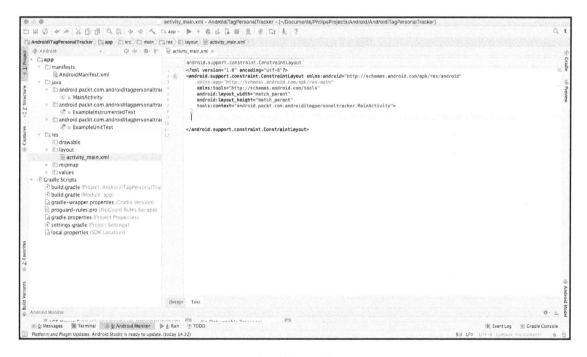

Figure 5: Activity UI XML

2. If you are using Android Studio 2.3.1 or upwards, then the UI XML by default should be initialized with `ConstraintLayout` as a root element of your UI:

```
<android.support.constraint.ConstraintLayout
xmlns:android="http://schemas.android.com/apk/res/android"
 xmlns:app="http://schemas.android.com/apk/res-auto"
 xmlns:tools="http://schemas.android.com/tools"
 android:layout_width="match_parent"
 android:layout_height="match_parent"
tools:context="android.packt.com.androiditagpersonaltracker.MainAct
ivity">
```

`ConstraintLayout` is a new `ViewGroup` introduced by Android as a separate support library. It is initialized as the default UI root element for each empty activity you initialize via Android Studio version 2.3.1 and upwards.

 If you do not know (yet) how `ConstraintLayout` works in Android, then do not sweat. There are plenty of resources out there which can help in understanding the internals of `ConstraintLayout`, the most popular being the Android developer website https://developer.android.com/training/constraint-layout/index.html.

In a `ConstraintLayout`, emphasis is given to creating the UI via the visual editor rather than the traditional way of editing the XML file.

3. Now, we shall add two buttons (one to start the scan and another to stop it) and a `ListView` (to display a list of devices found) to `ConstraintLayout` and we shall do this by editing `ConstraintLayout` directly in the in-built editor. For this, click on the **Design** button under the bottom-left corner of the XML editor. This should bring up the visual UI editor as shown in the following screenshot:

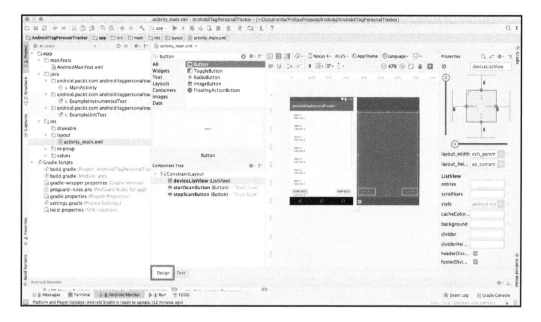

Figure 6: Visual UI Editor in Android Studio

Proceed to add two buttons and a `ListView` at positions shown in the preceding figure. This is relatively simple and if you struggle then we suggest you to go over the documentation/training for `ConstraintLayout` given on Android Developer website, which we mentioned in Step 2.

4. Once you have added the `ListView` and the buttons, then your XML should contain the following XML code for the `ListView`:

```
<ListView
  android:id="@+id/deviceListView"
  android:layout_width="match_parent"
  android:layout_height="wrap_content"
  android:layout_marginBottom="8dp"
  android:layout_marginLeft="8dp"
  android:layout_marginRight="8dp"
  android:layout_marginTop="8dp"
  app:layout_constraintBottom_toBottomOf="parent"
  app:layout_constraintHorizontal_bias="0.0"
  app:layout_constraintLeft_toLeftOf="parent"
  app:layout_constraintRight_toRightOf="parent"
  app:layout_constraintTop_toTopOf="parent"
  app:layout_constraintVertical_bias="0.0" />
```

It should also contain the following code for two buttons:

```xml
<Button
  android:id="@+id/startScanButton"
  android:layout_width="wrap_content"
  android:layout_height="wrap_content"
  android:layout_marginBottom="8dp"
  android:layout_marginLeft="8dp"
  android:text="Start Scan"
  app:layout_constraintBottom_toBottomOf="parent"
  app:layout_constraintLeft_toLeftOf="parent" />

<Button
  android:id="@+id/stopScanButton"
  android:layout_width="wrap_content"
  android:layout_height="wrap_content"
  android:layout_marginBottom="8dp"
  android:layout_marginRight="8dp"
  android:text="Stop Scan"
  app:layout_constraintBottom_toBottomOf="parent"
  app:layout_constraintRight_toRightOf="parent" />
```

These buttons will give us the ability to start and stop the process of scanning BLE Peripheral Devices and `ListView` will display the list of devices found.

5. As we did for the service explorer app in the `Chapter 3`, *Building a Service Explorer App*, we will need to define some permissions in the `AndroidManifest.xml` file:

```xml
<uses-permission android:name="android.permission.BLUETOOTH" />
<uses-permission android:name="android.permission.BLUETOOTH_ADMIN"
/>
<uses-permission
android:name="android.permission.ACCESS_COARSE_LOCATION" />
<uses-permission
android:name="android.permission.ACCESS_FINE_LOCATION" />
```

We have already created some UI and provided the necessary permissions to our app. Now we will add the necessary code to discover the iTag devices. It is important to first discover the iTag, connect with it, and then read the RSSI value, which then needs to be converted to distance. We now move to code this functionality.

Firstly, to control our UI elements (two Buttons and a `ListView`), we will need to access them in code. This can be done with the help of the following steps:

1. Please declare the `startScanningButton`, `stopScanningButton`, `deviceListView`, `listAdapter` and `deviceList` in the `MainActivity` class in the **MainActivity.java** file as shown in Chapter 3, *Building a Service Explorer App*. Please note that since our initial UI is exactly similar to the one in Chapter 3, *Building a Service Explorer App*, our UI initialization code is the same as and therefore, we won't be repeating it here. Please refer to **Steps 1 to 5** in under the *Application Code* Section in the Android App Design in Chapter 3, *Building a Service Explorer App*, to declare the aforementioned variables and initialise those in the `onCreate` method in the same way as we did earlier.

   > Our UI initialization is done and it is ready to interact via code. Now we will go ahead and define these member variables, which will help us to interact with Bluetooth Stack and the Bluetooth Low Energy hardware on the Android device. I request that you pay close attention from here onwards because we are about to cover the real core of our app:

2. We start by declaring the following member variables to manage our Bluetooth Low Energy functionality:

   ```
   BluetoothManager bluetoothManager;
   BluetoothAdapter bluetoothAdapter;
   BluetoothLeScanner bluetoothLeScanner;
   BluetoothGatt bluetoothGatt;
   ```

3. After declaring these Bluetooth Low Energy related member variables, we can initialize them as shown below in the `initialiseBluetooth` function, and add the function call in the `onCreate` method:

   ```
   private void initialiseBluetooth() {
   bluetoothManager =
   (BluetoothManager)getSystemService(Context.BLUETOOTH_SERVICE);
   bluetoothAdapter = bluetoothManager.getAdapter();
   bluetoothLeScanner = bluetoothAdapter.getBluetoothLeScanner();
   }
   ```

We will now add definitions for the `startScanning()` and `stopScanning()` functions.

4. Since we have the member variables for interacting with Bluetooth Low Energy functionality initialized, add the following definition to these functions for giving the aforementioned methods a body. The `startScanning()` and `stopScanning()` functions are performing the same functions as described in the Chapter 3, *Building a Service Explorer App*:

```
public void startScanning() {
listAdapter.clear();
deviceList.clear();
startScanningButton.setVisibility(View.INVISIBLE);
stopScanningButton.setVisibility(View.VISIBLE);
AsyncTask.execute(new Runnable() { @Override public void run()
{ bluetoothLeScanner.startScan(leScanCallback); } });
}

public void stopScanning() {
startScanningButton.setVisibility(View.VISIBLE);
stopScanningButton.setVisibility(View.INVISIBLE);
AsyncTask.execute(new Runnable() { @Override public void run()
{ bluetoothLeScanner.stopScan(leScanCallback); } });
}
```

5. The `BluetoothLEScanner` requires a callback function, which will be called for every device found and the devices found will be delivered as results to this call back, which we will define as follows:

```
// Device scan callback.
private ScanCallback leScanCallback = new ScanCallback() {
 @Override
 public void onScanResult(int callbackType, ScanResult result)
 {
   if (result.getDevice() != null) {
    if (!isDuplicate(result.getDevice())) {
     synchronized(result.getDevice()) {
      if (result.getDevice().getName() != null &&
result.getDevice().getName().toLowerCase().contains(NAME_iTAG))
{
        listAdapter.add(result.getDevice().getName());
        deviceList.add(result.getDevice());
      }
     }
    }
   }
 }
};
```

6. Inside the `ScanCallback`, `onScanResult` will be called for each device discovered. Since most of the iTag devices have a predefined name (which is some variant of iTag in most cases) to filter out just the iTag devices, we define it in our class:

```
private static final String NAME_iTAG = "itag";
```

In our custom implementation of the `onScanResult` method, we filter out the duplicates and append the filter results to the list. A part of the filtering logic is in the `isDuplicate()` method:

```
private boolean isDuplicate(BluetoothDevice device){
for(int i = 0; i < listAdapter.getCount(); i++) {
String addedDeviceDetail = listAdapter.getItem(i);
if(addedDeviceDetail.equals(device.getAddress()) ||
addedDeviceDetail.equals(device.getName())) { return true; } }
return false;
}
```

7. Once we have a list of iTags, we should be able to connect to an iTag and request its RSSI value. For this functionality, we will add a list item click listener on to each of our list items in the `onCreate` method as shown next so that we can connect to the device and read the RSSI when the list item corresponding to that device is clicked:

```
deviceListView.setOnItemClickListener(new
AdapterView.OnItemClickListener() {
@Override public void onItemClick(AdapterView<?> parent, View
view, int position, long id) {
stopScanning();
listAdapter.clear();
BluetoothDevice device = deviceList.get(position);
device.connectGatt(MainActivity.this, true, gattCallback); }
});
```

The listener listens for the click on the item on the list and on click stops scanning, cleans the list, and connects to the iTag represented by that list item.

8. Once you click on an iTag list item, a gatt connection attempt will be initiated via the `connectGatt` method. The `connectGatt` method requires a `BluetoothGattCallback`, where the results of connection state changes would be delivered asynchronously. This can be defined as follows:

```
protected BluetoothGattCallback gattCallback = new
BluetoothGattCallback() {
```

```
@Override
public void onConnectionStateChange(BluetoothGatt gatt, int
status, int newState) {
super.onConnectionStateChange(gatt, status, newState);
if (newState == BluetoothGatt.STATE_CONNECTED) {
Log.i(TAG, "onConnectionStateChange() - STATE_CONNECTED");
bluetoothGatt = gatt;
//Start a timer here
timer = new Timer();
timer.scheduleAtFixedRate(new TimerTask() {
@Override
public void run() {
//Called each time when 5000 milliseconds (5 seconds) (the
period parameter)
boolean rssiStatus = bluetoothGatt.readRemoteRssi();
}
},
//Set how long before to start calling the TimerTask (in
milliseconds)
0,
//Set the amount of time between each execution (in
milliseconds)
5000);
} else if (newState == BluetoothGatt.STATE_DISCONNECTED) {
Log.i(TAG, "onConnectionStateChange() - STATE_DISCONNECTED");
timer.cancel();
timer = null;
}
}
};
```

The preceding code contains some of the very important functionality related to the app; that is, if a successful connection occurs between the mobile device and the iTag, then onConnectionStateChange would be called with the updated state of the connection. We check the updated state (referred to as newState in the preceding code) and if the mobile device has connected successfully with the iTag, then we attempt to read the RSSI with this piece of code: bluetoothGatt.readRemoteRssi(). Also, we do this via a timer so that we can repeat the read operation in every 5 seconds. You will also need to declare a Timer variable as Timer timer; in this class, for the preceding code to compile successfully.

9. In the previous step, `GattCallback` received the updates for connection state changes and once the device is connected, we instruct it to fetch the RSSI value from the device through the callback itself. However, since the read operation is asynchronous, we need to override the `onReadRemoteRssi()` method to get the result of the RSSI reading:

```
@Override
public void onReadRemoteRssi(BluetoothGatt gatt, int rssi, int
status) {
  if (status == BluetoothGatt.GATT_SUCCESS) {
  Log.d(TAG, String.format("BluetoothGatt ReadRssi[%d]", rssi));
  Log.i(TAG, "Distance is: " + getDistance(rssi, 1));
  }
}
```

The RSSI read result will be delivered in the preceding callback. If you notice closely, after getting the RSSI value, we are calling the `getDistance` method with RSSI and one other mystery parameter. What does this method do and how is it implemented? We answer these questions in the next point.

10. If you recall our previous discussions, we mentioned that we would be making use of research papers to come up with an algorithm which converts RSSI to distance. We used the research paper mentioned below.

To learn about the intricacies of converting RSSI to distance, please navigate to `http://s2is.org/Issues/v1/n2/papers/paper14.pdf`.

With the above mentioned research paper we came up with the following method, which takes in the RSSI and TxPower and converts them to the distance of the device from the iTag in meters. RSSI-based localization is a hot topic still under constant research and the following is one of the most popular formulas out there today to convert RSSI with graceful approximation:

```
double getDistance(int rssi, int txPower) {
    /*
    * RSSI = TxPower - 10 * n * lg(d)
    * n is usually 2 or 4 in free space
    *
    * d = 10 ^ ((TxPower - RSSI) / (10 * n))
    */
    return (Math.pow(10d, ((double) txPower - rssi) / (10 *
4)))/10;
}
```

Note that we call the preceding method once we receive the current RSSI value and the function call happens like this: `getDistance(rssi, 1)`. The first parameter is obviously the RSSI, the second mystery parameter is the TxPower output of the iTag as mentioned here.

> To read about the technical specifications of an iTag, visit `https://fccid.io/2ABQE-ITAG`.

As per the description provided on the preceding link, the TxPower output of the iTag is 1.25 mW, which is almost 1 dbm.

> You can use this link to convert mW to dBm `http://www.rapidtables.com/convert/power/mW_to_dBm.htm`.

Hence, the 1 as the second parameter in the method call to `getDistance`.

11. It might very well happen that when the user starts our app, they have their Bluetooth turned off. In such a case, the app shall prompt them to turn it on. Add this piece of code in the `onCreate` method:

```
if (bluetoothAdapter != null && !bluetoothAdapter.isEnabled())
{
 Intent enableIntent = new
Intent(BluetoothAdapter.ACTION_REQUEST_ENABLE);
 startActivityForResult(enableIntent, REQUEST_ENABLE_BT);
}
```

We also need to handle security. Android M onwards, we need to declare location permissions in the manifest as well as a request at runtime, which is done by the following code.

12. Add the following code to the `onCreate` method:

```
if
(this.checkSelfPermission(Manifest.permission.ACCESS_COARSE_LOC
ATION) != PackageManager.PERMISSION_GRANTED) {
 final AlertDialog.Builder builder = new
AlertDialog.Builder(this);
 builder.setTitle("This app needs location access");
 builder.setMessage("Please grant location access so this app
can detect peripherals.");
```

```
builder.setPositiveButton(android.R.string.ok, null);
builder.show();
}
```

Now, it is time to run the app and see what happens. As soon as you launch the app and if your Bluetooth is turned off, the app will ask you if it can turn the Bluetooth on.

Once you have allowed it, the second thing the app will point out is that it needs location access. Following the location dialog, you can exit the app or send it in the background, then enable location on the device and also navigate to **Settings** | **Apps** | **Permissions** and enable the **Location Permission** for the app itself.

Once you have enabled location and allowed location access, you can come back to the app and click on the **Scan** button:

Figure 7: Discovery Results after pressing the Scan button

The app should display a list of Bluetooth Low Energy iTag devices in the vicinity (if any). Our app is intelligent enough to filter and display the name of iTag device(s) only.

13. If you tap on the iTag device found in the last step, nothing should happen on the screen; however, if you look at the logs in the Android monitor, then you should see the following statements occurring continuously at a fixed interval of 5 seconds:

android.packt.com.androiditagpersonaltracker D/PacktBLEiTag: BluetoothGatt ReadRssi[-89]
android.packt.com.androiditagpersonaltracker I/PacktBLEiTag: Distance is: 1.7782794100389228

The first statement represents the current RSSI value and the second statement represents the distance calculated from that RSSI value. Although we are now calculating the distance, it would be good to show it to the user too. For this, update the onReadRemoteRssi method to the following code:

```
@Override
public void onReadRemoteRssi(BluetoothGatt gatt, int rssi, int status) {
  if (status == BluetoothGatt.GATT_SUCCESS) {
  Log.d(TAG, String.format("BluetoothGatt ReadRssi[%d]", rssi));
  double distance = getDistance(rssi, 1);
  Log.i(TAG, "Distance is: " + distance);
  if (distanceList.size() == MAX_DISTANCE_VALUES) {
  double sum = 0;
  for (int i = 0; i < MAX_DISTANCE_VALUES; i++) {
  sum = sum + distanceList.get(i);
  }
  final double averageDistance = sum / MAX_DISTANCE_VALUES;
  distanceList.clear();
  showToast("iTag is " + averageDistance + " mts. away");
  } else {
  showToast("Gathering Data");
  distanceList.add(distance);
  }
}}
```

You may recall from our earlier discussions, that we pointed out that RSSI is a trend and fluctuates a lot. In our modified `onReadRemoteRssi` method, we attempt to nullify this fluctuation by taking an average of 10 distance values. Also, while we collect the 10 values to be taken, we inform the user by continuously showing a toast to the user mentioning that we are **Gathering Data**:

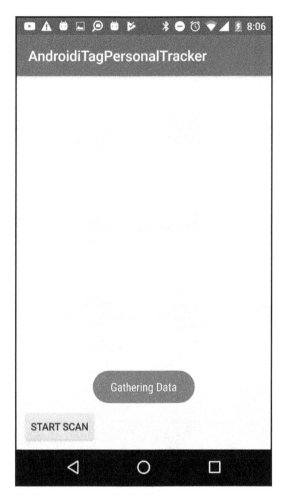

Figure 8: Gathering RSSI Data

Once we have all the 10 values, we can calculate the final distance via averaging and show it to the user:

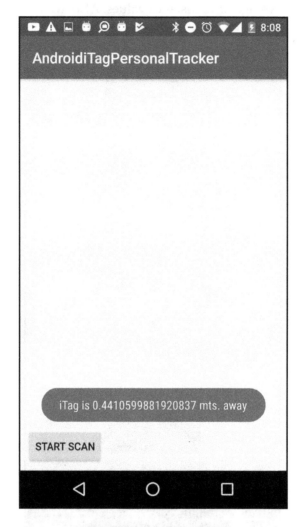

Figure 9: Distance calculation and display

After this, discard the previous values and start afresh for the next round of 10 values.

We use the following method to show the toast:

```
final void showToast(final String message) {
runOnUiThread(new Runnable() {
@Override
public void run() {
Toast.makeText(MainActivity.this, message, Toast.LENGTH_SHORT).show();
}
});
}
```

We will also need to declare the following variables for our code to compile successfully:

```
ArrayList<Double> distanceList = new ArrayList<>();
private final static int MAX_DISTANCE_VALUES = 10;
```

Now that we are reading the RSSI data, all that remains is to upload it to a server so that it can be remotely accessible to anyone who wants to read/access it. For this, we will integrate Firebase into our Android app and upload the distance measurements to the Firebase Cloud:

1. To integrate Firebase into the app, we will follow the same steps that we used in Chapter 3, *Building a Service Explorer App*, using the Firebase Assistant:

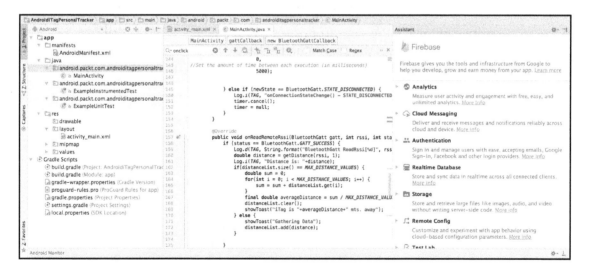

Figure 10: Setting up Firebase using the Firebase Assistant

2. Make sure you give this app a distinguishing name as shown in the following screenshot, so that we do not collide with our other Apps on the Firebase Cloud instance:

Figure 11: Creating a new Firebase Project

3. Continue following the steps from Chapter 3, *Building a Service Explorer App*, until you connect the app to the Firebase cloud, which will be indicated by the green button shown in the following screenshot in the Firebase Assistant:

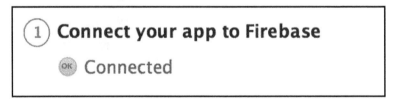

Figure 12: Firebase App Connection Status

4. Once you have connected the app, click on the second item in the assistant window, which says **Add the Realtime Database to your app**, which is again very similar to what we saw in `Chapter 3`, *Building a Service Explorer App*:

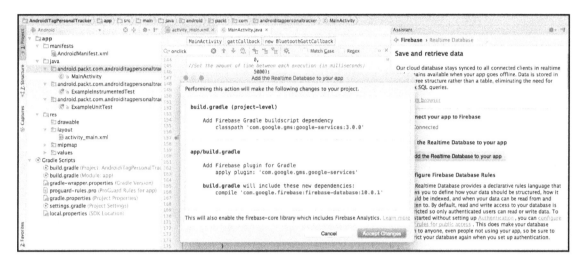

Figure 13: Adding Firebase to the Project

5. Finally, after all the setup, click on **Configure your rules for public access** under step 3 in the assistant window. This step will open the browser with some Firebase documentation.

6. Click on **Go to Console** on the top-right corner of this screen. This will open up a dashboard/gallery of existing applications.

7. Choose the relevant application name; in our case, it is
   `AndroidiTagPersonalTracker`, as shown in the following screenshot:

Figure 14: Firebase Apps Console

8. You should be taken to a detailed console. From here, click on **Database** in the
   left pane and select the **Rules** tab from the list of horizontal tabs.

9. What you should be seeing in front of you is a JSON file signifying rules as key-
   value pairs:

   1. Change the `.read` key from `auth != null` to `true`.
   2. Do the same for the `.write` key.
   3. Hit the **Publish** button on the top.

   Note that this configuration is for demo purposes only, which means anyone can
   read or write to your database. In the real world, your rules will be more
   advanced and sophisticated than this.

10. Once you have made the changes, in our Android app, in the
    `onReadRemoteRssi` method, add the following code to send the data to the
    cloud:

    ```
    // Write a message to the database
    FirebaseDatabase database = FirebaseDatabase.getInstance();
    DatabaseReference myRef = database.getReference("proximity");
    myRef.setValue(new Double(averageDistance).toString());
    ```

This code needs to be added just below the following line in the `onReadRemoteRssi` method:

```
distanceList.clear()
```

11. Run our Android app, discover the iTag and connect to read the RSSI values.
12. Navigate to the Firebase Console and Voila! Under the **DATA** tab, you should see the value of distance/proximity being updated on the console:

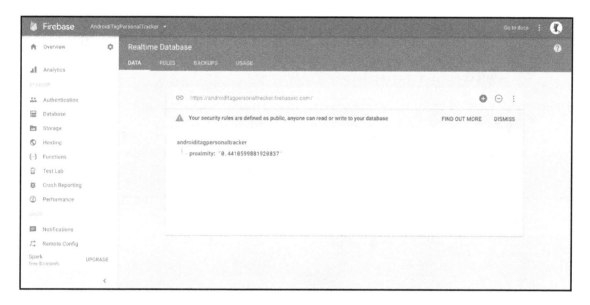

Figure 15: Proximity data successfully uploaded to Firebase backend by the App

Now, this value is available to be remotely monitored for anyone who is interested in monitoring the proximity of the device/person on which the iTag is planted. Also, the value will update itself dynamically once every 5 seconds.

As an exercise, you can try modifying the code of the App to send remote notifications via email/message, if the distance value goes up by a specific threshold.

All the code for what we covered in this section is available on the GitHub link mentioned next.

For Android iTag Tracker App's Code, visit `https://github.com/madhurbhargava/AndroidiTagPersonalTracker`.

Let's move to iOS now.

iOS

For iOS, we begin the same way as we did with Android, with an empty project. We name our app `iOSiTagPersonalTracker` and get started with project creation as described in `Chapter 3`, *Building a Service Explorer App*.

 To run on an actual device, you will need to create an Apple ID and generate a signing certificate associated with that ID. You can find the complete process at `http://blog.ionic.io/deploying-to-a-device-without-an-apple-developer-account/`.

To keep you focused on core concepts, we will keep our iOS app as simple as possible:

1. We start by creating an empty project by the name `iOSiTagPersonalTracker`. If the project creation was successful, then you should be presented with the project in Xcode as shown in the following screenshot:

Figure 16: iOSBLEServiceExplorer App in Xcode

You should be presented with a list of files as shown in the **Project Navigator**—the major ones being **ViewController.swift**, **Main.storyboard**, and **AppDelegate.swift**. We will be mainly interacting with the ViewController for the logic.

We will take a slightly different approach this time as compared to Android while interacting with the nearby Bluetooth Low Energy devices via iOS. In Android, we used to display a list of devices found to the user and then let the user decide which device he/she wanted to explore in terms of services and characteristics. In iOS, we will connect to each device as it is discovered and explore its services and characteristics while also displaying the findings to the user. Sounds fun? Let's code this:

1. Apart from adding a CBCentralManager member like we did in Chapter 3, *Building a BLE Service Explorer App,* we shall also define a name variable for the iTag for filtering purposes and add those to the ViewController class as shown below:

   ```
   var manager:CBCentralManager!
   let NAME_iTag = "itag"
   var iTagPeripheral:CBPeripheral!
   ```

   CBCentralManager objects are used to manage discovered and connected peripheral (CBPeripheral) objects.

2. Initialize the CBCentralManager object in the viewDidLoad method of the ViewController as follows:

   ```
   override func viewDidLoad() { super.viewDidLoad()
   manager = CBCentralManager(delegate: self, queue: nil)
   }
   ```

   We need to adapt our ViewController to the protocol as we need the results of the discovery process. Consider the methods of the CBCentralManagerDelegate similar to the callbacks (gattCallback) that we defined in our earlier Android code.

3. Please adapt ViewController to the CBCentralManagerDelegate protocol as shown next:

   ```
   class ViewController: UIViewController,
   CBCentralManagerDelegate
   ```

4. We need to set the delegate for `CBCentralManager`:

```
manager.delegate = self
```

5. We track the state of the `CBCentralManager` in
   the `centralManagerDidUpdateState` method. We start scanning for devices as
   soon as it is in `poweredOn` state as shown next:

```
func centralManagerDidUpdateState(_ central: CBCentralManager)
{ if central.state == .poweredOn {
central.scanForPeripherals(withServices: nil, options: nil) }
else { print("Bluetooth not available.") }
}
```

We are essentially instructing the manager to find all the advertising peripherals
without any filtering.

6. Please implement the following method to receive results of the scan:

```
public func centralManager(_ central: CBCentralManager,
didDiscover peripheral: CBPeripheral, advertisementData:
[String : Any], rssi RSSI: NSNumber) {
 let device = (advertisementData as NSDictionary)
 .object(forKey: CBAdvertisementDataLocalNameKey)
 as? String
 if let device = device {
 let trimmedDeviceName = device.trimmingCharacters(in:
.whitespacesAndNewlines)
 if trimmedDeviceName.caseInsensitiveCompare(NAME_iTag) ==
.orderedSame {
 iTagPeripheral = peripheral
 manager.connect(iTagPeripheral, options: nil)
 }
 }
}
```

The preceding method is from the `CBCentralManagerDelegate` class, which we adopted in step 3. Unlike Android, we will filter the devices based on their names and initiate connection to the first iTag device found.

If `CBCentralManager` is able to connect to the iTag successfully, then the following method will be called via the delegate:

```
public func centralManager(_ central: CBCentralManager,
didConnect peripheral: CBPeripheral) {
        iTagPeripheral.delegate = self
        iTagPeripheral.readRSSI()
    }
```

In the preceding method, which would be called if the connection to iTag was successful, we try to read the RSSI value asynchronously. Just like the `CBCentralManager` object, the `CBPeripheral` object needs a delegate to report the results of the asynchronous operation.

Hence, we shall adapt our `ViewController` class to the `CBPeripheralDelegate` object as shown next:

```
class ViewController: UIViewController, CBCentralManagerDelegate,
CBPeripheralDelegate
```

Now, our `ViewController` class is going to receive updates for both actions taken by the central as well as the peripheral.

As and when the RSSI read is done, the peripheral will report its results to the delegate's method mentioned next:

```
func peripheral(_ peripheral: CBPeripheral, didReadRSSI RSSI: NSNumber,
error: Error?) {
        showToast(message: "Distance from iTag: \(calculateDistance(rssi:
RSSI.intValue, txPower: 1)) mts.")
    }
```

We are using a little bit of Android Jargon here. A *toast* on Android is the name given to a popup message that shows up briefly and finally fades away. iOS does not have toasts, hence keeping our UI the same on both platforms, we will implement our own custom toast message for iOS via the `showToast` method as demonstrated later.

Meanwhile, please pay close attention to the preceding code, which does two important things. Firstly, it calculates the distance in a manner similar to that we employed on Android using the following function:

```swift
func calculateDistance(rssi:Int,txPower:Int) -> Double {
    /*
     * RSSI = TxPower - 10 * n * lg(d)
     * n = 2 (in free space)
     *
     * d = 10 ^ ((TxPower - RSSI) / (10 * n))
     */
    let result = pow(10.0, (txPower - rssi) / (10 * 4))
    return NSDecimalNumber(decimal: result).doubleValue/10.0
}
```

Secondly, it shows the calculated value on the screen via the `showToast` method.

```swift
extension UIViewController {
    func showToast(message : String) {
        let toastLabel = UILabel(frame: CGRect(x:
self.view.frame.size.width/2 - 125, y: self.view.frame.size.height-100,
width: 250, height: 35))
        toastLabel.backgroundColor = UIColor.black.withAlphaComponent(0.6)
        toastLabel.textColor = UIColor.white
        toastLabel.textAlignment = .center;
        toastLabel.font = UIFont(name: "Helvetica-Bold", size: 16.0)
        toastLabel.text = message
        toastLabel.alpha = 1.0
        toastLabel.layer.cornerRadius = 10;
        toastLabel.clipsToBounds = true
        self.view.addSubview(toastLabel)
        UIView.animate(withDuration: 14.0, delay: 0.1, options:
.curveEaseOut, animations: {
            toastLabel.alpha = 0.0
        }, completion: {(isCompleted) in
            toastLabel.removeFromSuperview()
        })
    }
}
```

Notice that in the preceding code, rather than creating the method in the same class, we created it as an extension.

 To read more about extensions, Please visit: `https://developer.apple.com/library/content/documentation/Swift/Conceptual/Swift_Programming_Language/Extensions.html`

And, we are done. If you launch the app, and have a broadcasting iTag nearby, then it should automatically connect and show the distance from the broadcasting iTag as shown in the following screenshot:

Figure 17: App Launch

We are done with the basic framework to build the proximity app on iOS. All the code that we discussed in this section is available on the link mentioned next.

 For iOS iTag Personal Tracker App's Code, visit `https://github.com/madhurbhargava/iOSiTagPersonalTracker.`

As an exercise, you can start extending the app from here and make it similar to Android by adding a richer user interface, repeated polling, and uploading data to the backend.

Summary

In this chapter we took the road less traveled, and by using an iTag in a nontraditional manner, we ended up building a Bluetooth Low Energy based proximity solution. Apart from the overall technical implementation, another important detail worth mentioning is the fact that we executed our code of the Android App on a Samsung Galaxy S8 device (alongside with LG Nexus 5), which is a very special device in today's market due to the fact that it is the only device that supports BLE 5 available at the time of writing. We recommend that you do run the examples presented in this book on a device that supports BLE 5, since this will help you gauge the important practical differences between the older and relatively newer BLE versions. Also, we request that you follow up both the Android and iOS examples with the homework exercises outlined in the individual sections. This will not only strengthen your overall solid grounding in Bluetooth Low Energy, but will also help with a better understanding of the topic at hand.

As we are progressing, we are slowly building our understanding of how and why Bluetooth Low Energy will impact IoT. After this chapter, we have already connected at least two distinct sensor types to the internet and made their data available to remote monitoring.

In Chapter 5, *Beacons with Raspberry Pi*, we shall explore an important cornerstone of Bluetooth Low Energy technology, that is, beacons. As we always do, rather than buying a premade solution and playing around with that, we shall build our own beacon from ground up using a DIY Raspberry Pi board.

5

Beacons with Raspberry Pi

The technology you use impresses no one. The experience you create with it is everything.

- Sean Gerety

In the last chapter, we brewed our very own indoor positioning system by using nothing more than a smartphone, an iTag, and a few brilliantly written research papers. Building on our knowledge about discovering and connecting with Bluetooth Low Energy devices from the previous chapters, we discovered that apart from services and characteristics, there is much more that Bluetooth Low Energy has to offer; for instance, we used RSSI to extract relevant information from a Bluetooth Low Energy device by converting it to proximity/distance.

This chapter is a little different from the previous ones. Building on our knowledge of implementation details that we gathered in the previous chapters, rather than introducing a new implementation detail, this chapter introduces the reader to a completely new class of Bluetooth Low Energy devices, that is, Beacons.

We will be covering the following topics to create solid understanding about Beacons:

- Introduction to Beacons
- Introduction to Raspberry Pi
- Creating a Beacon with Raspberry Pi
- Writing an App to Detect the Beacon

Despite a variety of Beacons being easily available in the market, we shall resort to building our own using a Raspberry Pi, which is a small single board computing device, so as to get a better understanding of what goes under the hood of a Beaconing device.

Let's get started.

Introduction to Beacons

Stating simply, a Beacon is a small wireless device, which transmits continuous radio/Bluetooth Low Energy signals. Depending on the *protocol* being used, these signals package contextual information, which can then be intercepted by nearby Bluetooth Low Energy devices (which in most cases are smart phones), and then depending on the context and use case, the intercepted information is either presented to the user or sent to a backend for further processing or both.

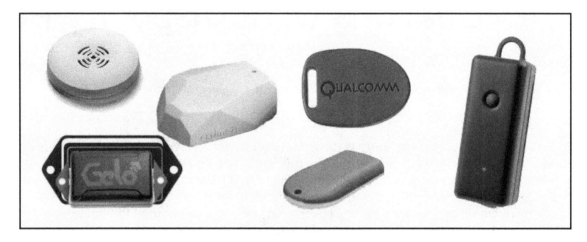

Figure 1: Various types of Beacons

Apart from the hardware itself, a protocol plays an important role and is one of the fundamental building blocks of any Beacon-related application use case. In very simple words, for the purpose of wireless communication, a protocol is a set of rules defining data transmission in a wireless channel.

 Do not get confused between a protocol and the Beacon itself. A Beacon is a piece of hardware whereas a protocol is the way in which data is structured and transmitted by Beacons. Just for the sake of clarity, if a Beacon was analogous to a person, then a protocol would be the language that the person speaks.

Beacons and related protocols have become so important and mainstream that Google and Apple have come up with their own protocols for Beacon-based transmissions, which are as follows:

- **iBeacon**: This is a protocol developed by Apple
- **Eddystone**: This is a protocol developed by Google

We shall delve into the details of these protocols just in a short while.

Information transfer via Beacons is widely applied to a variety of use cases as shown in the following figure:

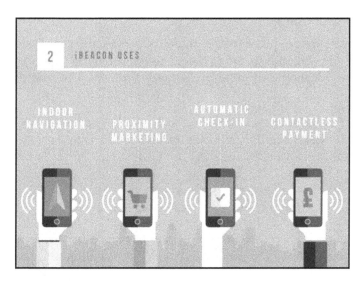

Figure 2: Usages of Beacons in a retail store; source: www.vendhq.com

Brick and mortar retail stores use the Beacons for mobile commerce, offering customers special deals through mobile marketing, and can enable mobile payments through point-of-sale systems. The following figure illustrates the complete life cycle of a retail-oriented use case for Beacons:

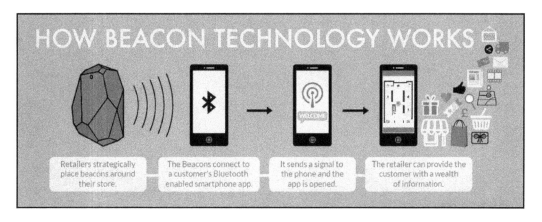

Figure 3: A retail use case of Beacons; Source: www.shopify.com

Among their many uses, indoor navigation and proximity marketing are two primary use cases of Beacons and not just these two but almost all beacon use cases rely on the proximity of the receiving device, hence based on its importance, we already identified and introduced the conversion of RSSI to proximity in the last chapter, which will serve as a foundation for this chapter.

 Beacons are unique since the signal/information transmission happens only one way (that is, from beacon to the receiving device), which in the communication terminology is known as **simplex communication**.

Coming back to our discussion regarding protocols, we shall cover both Eddystone and iBeacon in theory. However, for data transfer formats in the samples introduced in this chapter (for both Android and iOS), we shall use Eddystone.

Eddystone

As it is for everything Google or Android, Eddystone is an open source protocol specification by Google released in July 2015, which defines Bluetooth Low Energy message format specifically for Beacons. Unlike iBeacon, which is officially supported by iOS devices only, Eddystone has official support for both iOS and Android.

 To read and explore the Eddystone specification, visit `https://github.com/google/eddystone`.

The Eddystone protocol format has been named after the famous Eddystone lighthouse in the UK and defines four different message formats as shown as follows:

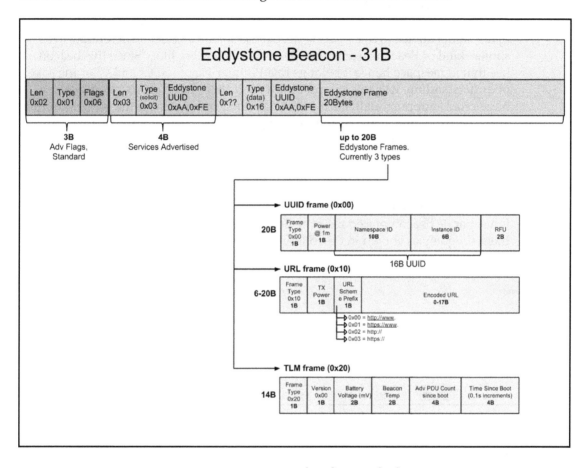

Figure 4: Eddystone Beacon Format (Source: developer.mbed.org)

We shall cover each message format in detail:

1. **Eddystone-UID**: Eddystone-UID is used to broadcast a 16-byte Beacon identifier. The 16-byte Beacon identifier is divided into two parts, namely, namespace (10 bytes) and instance (6 bytes). A namespace is something that differentiates similar kind of Beacons from other Beacons (something like, "Since this beacon has that namespace hence it belongs to a Popular Fast food Chain"). For the sake of understanding, let's say a popular fast food chain has 5 different outlets in a huge retail shopping mall. Each outlet has 2 beacons, one near the burger counter and 1 near the milk shake counter making it a collective of 10 beacons. Then all of those 10 Beacons will have a similar namespace ID, since they all belong to a similar context(same fast food company). However, each of those 10 Beacons will have different instance ID (something like, "Since this beacon has that Namespace hence it belongs to a Popular Fast food Chain and since it has this Instance ID hence it belongs to that shop near the Milkshake Counter. For the burgers, there is a separate beacon placed near the Burger Counter."), so as to identify each of them uniquely as shown in the following figure:

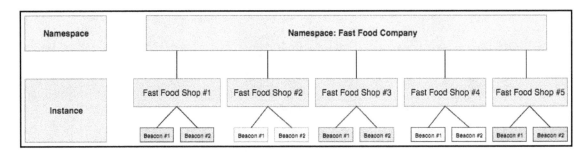

Figure 5: Namespace and Instance in Eddystone UUID format

2. **Eddystone-URL**: The EddyStone-URL packet consists of a single URL field used to broadcast a URL, as shown previously in the figure indicating the beacon format, which can then navigate the user to any website that has SSL security. These URLs form the backbone of something known as **Physical Web**, a platform using which Google plans to convert Internet of things to Internet of any thing.

To read more about Physical Web, visit `http://google.github.io/physical-web/`.

3. **Eddystone-TLM**: Eddystone-TLM packet broadcasts telemetry information about the Beacon itself. The telemetry packet consists of the following:

   - Battery voltage: This can be used to estimate the battery level of a beacon
   - Beacon temperature: This is the number of packets sent since the beacon was last powered-up or rebooted
   - Beacon uptime: The is the time since last power-up or reboot

4. **Eddystone-EID**: Eddystone-EID is a time varying packet, somewhat similar to the UID packet, however, specifically designed for security against hijacking and spoofing.

iBeacon

iBeacon has been around since 2013, which was way before Google's Eddystone's protocol. Due to its early inception, it was also the first Beacon protocol to be introduced. Unlike Eddystone, iBeacon protocol is proprietary and the specification is controlled by Apple. iBeacon is a much more simpler protocol to implement as compared to Eddystone. iBeacon just defines a single message format with 31 bytes of data as shown in the following figure:

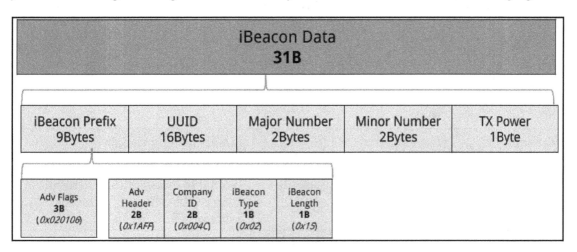

Figure 4: iBeacon advertisement packet

Each iBeacon packet consists of three important parts:

- A **Universally Unique Identifier** (**UUID**) that identifies the beacon as part of a large group (for example, "This Beacon belongs to a popular local Chain of Clothing Stores")

- A **Major Number** that narrows down the Beacon as part of a subgroup in the large group (for example, if an app identifies the UUID and Major of an iBeacon, then it can deduce the following information, "This beacon is located in the shop located in the Main Market of that Clothing Store Chain")

- A **Minor Number** that identifies a specific Beacon in that group (for example, if an app identifies the UUID and the Major and Minor of an iBeacon, then it can deduce the following information, "This Beacon is located in the shop located in the Main Market of the Clothing Store Chain near the entrance")

Since iBeacon (or even EddyStone for that instance) advertising packet contains specific information about where the Beacon is located, it becomes very easy to track movements of a user. This is usually done in co-ordination with an app. Since Beacons use simplex communication to make data available to their listeners/receivers, the app which receives and tracks this data can send it to the backend where it can be analyzed to produce results such as, in which section of a specific shop did the user spend most time or what was of user's interest the most.

So this was about iBeacon and Eddystone. We have outlined their major differences in the following table:

	iBeacon	**Eddystone**
Technology	Developed by Apple	Developed by Google
Compatibility	It is Android and iOS compatible, but native only for iOS.	It is Android and iOS compatible. In fact, it is cross-platform and thus is compatible with any platform that supports BLE Beacons.
Profile	It is a proprietary software. Thus, the specification is controlled by Apple.	It is open-source.

Ease of use	It is simple to implement.	It is flexible but requires more complicated coding when it comes to integration since it sends more packets of information than iBeacon.
Broadcasted packets	iBeacon broadcasts only one advertising packet.	Eddystone broadcasts four different packets: • Eddystone-UID • Eddystone-URL • Eddystone-TLM • Eddystone-EID
Security and Privacy	There is no specific feature such as **Ephemeral Identifiers** (**EIDs**) in iBeacon. The signal transmitted by a beacon is a public signal and can be detected by any iOS device and certain Android devices with proper specifications.	Eddystone has a built-in feature called EIDs that constantly changes and allows Beacons to broadcast a signal that can only be identified by authorized clients.

Given that you already have some idea about various beacon formats, we now introduce you to Raspberry Pi, a mini (ature) but very powerful computer, which we shall use to create our very first Eddystone-URL beacon.

Introduction to Raspberry Pi

For the purpose of introduction, Raspberry Pi is a series of small single board computers, created by Raspberry Pi Foundation in February 2012.

 To read more about Raspberry Pi Foundation, visit `https://www.raspberrypi.org/`.

The vision behind these miniature computers was to teach basic computer science in the schools in and around the UK and in various developing countries, which is identified by the mission of the Raspberry Pi Foundation, that is, "To put the power of digital making into the hands of people all over the world".

However, due to their low cost and longer durability, Raspberry Pi surpassed the anticipation of its makers by becoming hugely popular with hackers and novices alike. It further went on to become the best-selling PC in the UK of all time.

The following figure shows the timeline of the release of various models of Raspberry Pi up until 2015:

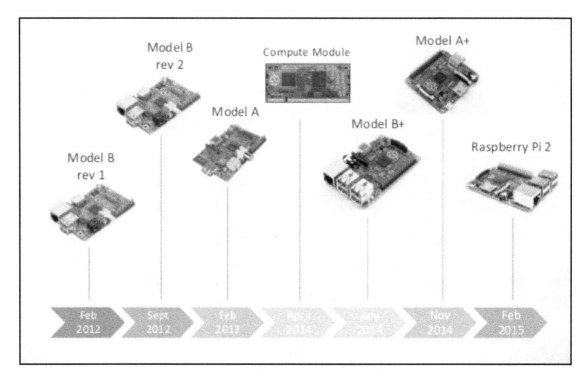

Figure 5: Timeline, the advent and evolution of Raspberry Pi

February 2016 marked the advent of a third generation Raspberry Pi Model 3B over Model 2B, which is the current latest Raspberry Pi in the market as of the time of writing this chapter and also the one which we would be using. To give you some idea about its prowess, the following are its specifications:

- Quad Core 1.2GHz Broadcom BCM2837 64bit CPU
- 1GB RAM
- BCM43438 wireless LAN and Bluetooth Low Energy (BLE) on board
- 40-pin extended GPIO
- 4 USB 2 ports
- 4 Pole stereo output and composite video port

- Full size HDMI
- CSI camera port for connecting a Raspberry Pi camera
- DSI display port for connecting a Raspberry Pi touchscreen display
- Micro SD port for loading your operating system and storing data
- Upgraded switched Micro USB power source up to 2.5A

All this on a board slightly bigger than the size of a credit card. Isn't it amazing?

Figure 6: Raspberry Pi, Size comparison; source: `www.digitaltrends.com`

Notice the specifications, there is a 64-bit Quad Core 1.2 GHz CPU and 1 GB of RAM there and much more, and the cost of all of this goodness is around 40 euros, which make it one of the most powerful and yet inexpensive computers ever sold.

If you are going to purchase a Raspberry Pi, it is better to go for a complete kit, which usually bundles the Raspberry Pi board itself, a power supply, an SD card with operating system installer as preinstalled, and a cover case. For the display, you can either use your old desktop PC's display or buy a smaller portable one online. For Input, any USB keyboard and mouse will work fine.

Raspberry Pi essentials Kit is one of the many popular kits available in the market, bundling the bare essentials to get you started. Its contents are shown in the following figure:

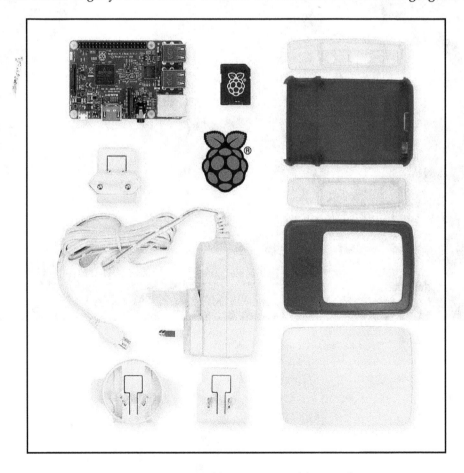

Figure 7: Raspberry Pi essentials Kit; source: www.wehkamp.nl

One of the good things about this kit is that it includes a 16-GB microSD card (also known as a NOOBS card) with **New Out Of the Box Software** (**NOOBS**) preinstalled in it. NOOBS , which is an operating system (OS) installer.

 To read more about NOOBS, visit `https://www.raspberrypi.org/downloads/noobs/`.

This OS installer already comes bundled with *Raspbian,* which is a free operating system based on *Debian,* which in turn is one of the earliest operating systems based on Linux kernel and hence contains a lot of goodies from the original Linux kernel.

 To know more about Debian, visit `https://www.debian.org/`.

Raspbian is specifically optimized to run on Raspberry Pi hardware and also the officially supported operating system by the Raspberry Pi Foundation.

 To know more about Raspbian, visit `https://www.raspbian.org/`.

Raspbian comes preinstalled with plenty of software for education, programming, and general use. It has Python, Scratch, Sonic Pi, Java, Mathematica, and more. We shall be building our beacon on top of Raspbian itself.

Creating a Beacon with Raspberry Pi

We shall be creating a Beacon on top of Raspbian and we would be doing that using one of the popular tools that come bundled with the original Linux kernel. We shall begin by setting up the Raspberry Pi (Model 3B) and we are assuming that you have a Raspberry Pi essentials kit, a keyboard, a mouse and a display (monitor) to start with:

1. Plug in the USB mouse and keyboard to the USB ports, also connect the monitor to the Pi via the HDMI cable. If you do not have an HDMI monitor, you can use the appropriate converter for the purpose. A port outline of the Raspberry Pi Model 3B is shown in the following image:

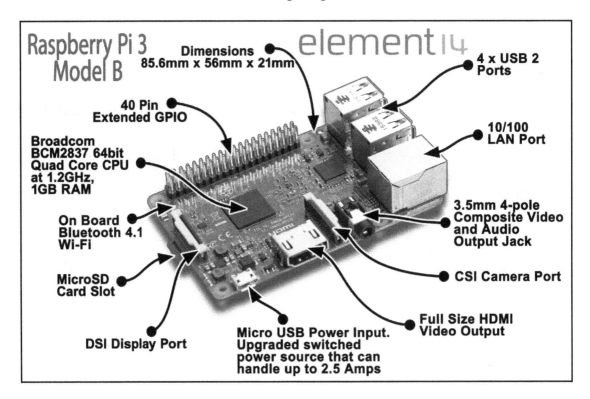

Figure 8: Ports on Raspberry Pi Model 3B; source: www.element14.com

2. Use the NOOBS card that came bundled with the essentials kit and insert it into the MicroSD card slot. Additionally, not essentially, you can also put up the housing/case over the Pi, which came bundled with the essentials kit.

3. We have hooked up all the I/O units, plus inserted the NOOBS card. Time to power up the Pi; the essentials kit contains a newly designed 2.5A AC adapter. Connect the adapter to the Micro USB power input. Also, the essentials kit has a lot of power heads covering all kinds of power supply sockets across the globe, so that you do not have to worry about which region you are based and buy a separate converter for that region. This is very handy since you can travel across the world without the need of various converting plugs.

4. The Pi does not have an on/off switch. Hence, as soon as you plug in the power adapter, it should be powered on.

5. As soon as the Pi boots up for the first time, you should eventually see a window indicating that the NOOBS installer has launched successfully.

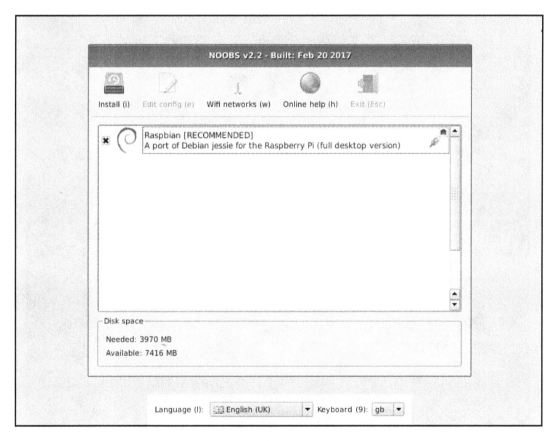

Figure 9: NOOBS Installer

Using the mouse, select the **Raspbian** as indicated in the preceding screenshot, if not already selected, and proceed to click on the **Install** button in the preceding bar. You should get a warning/confirmation dialog mentioning, that all data on the SD card will be overwritten. Fret not and click on **Yes** to begin the installation. The installation window should now come up and the installation should begin, which should roughly take around 15~20 minutes. Post installation, a dialog should come up stating that the installation has finished. Click on **Ok** on this dialog.

6. On clicking on **Ok**, the Raspberry Pi should start re-booting as shown in the following screenshot:

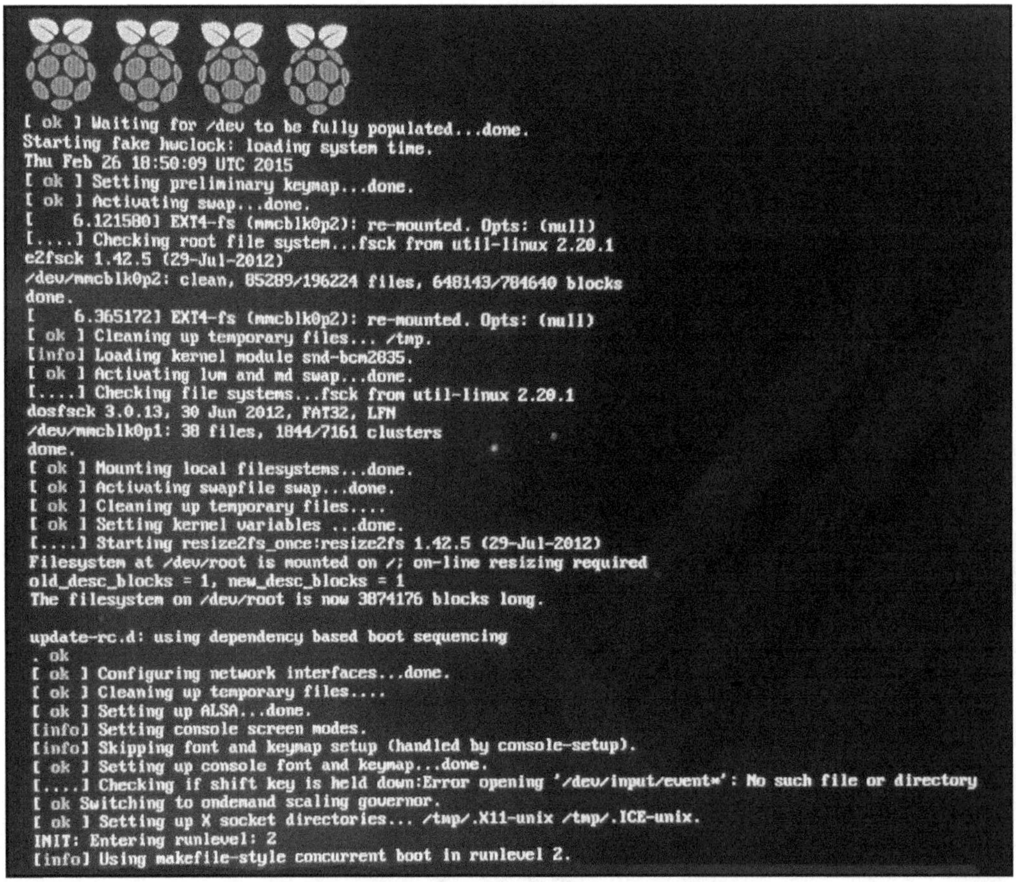

Figure 10: Raspberry Pi Rebooting; source: www.raspberrypi.org

After the boot-up has finished, you should see the Raspbian desktop with Raspberry Pi logo in the center:

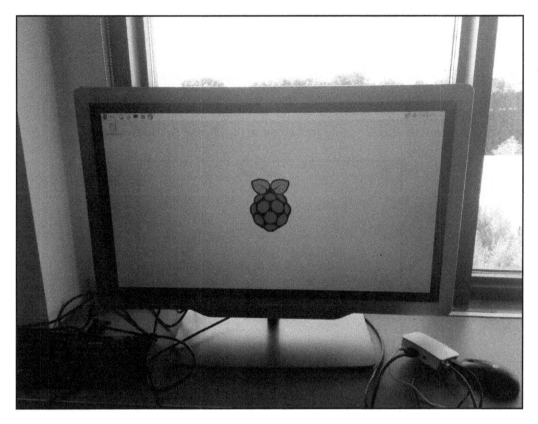

Figure 11: Raspbian Desktop

So far so good. We have successfully setup our Raspberry Pi to run Raspbian. Now, we shall use it to broadcast Eddystone advertisement packets. For this, we shall use a Linux utility/tool(s) `hciconfig` and `hcitool` respectively.

Raspberry Pi Model 3B already has onboard hardware for Bluetooth 4.1. We shall enable this hardware first with the use of `hciconfig` and then use `hcitool` to broadcast Eddystone advertisements.

 To read more about hciconfig, visit `https://linux.die.net/man/8/ hciconfig`.

1. The Raspbian desktop has a menubar on the top. Click on the **Menu** button on this menubar and navigate to **Accessories | Terminal**. Launch the terminal:

Figure 12: Raspbian Terminal Access

2. After the **Terminal** is launched, type the following command in the terminal to enable the Bluetooth hardware:

```
pi@raspberrypi:~ $ sudo hciconfig hci0 up
```

3. Since Beacons are non-connectable Bluetooth devices, which are just there to advertise, we shall instruct the Raspberry Pi Bluetooth hardware to be just advertising and non-connectable by the following command:

```
pi@raspberrypi:~ $ sudo hciconfig hci0 leadv 3
```

4. Provide the Beacon advertising data using `hcitool`:

```
$ sudo hcitool -i hci0 cmd 0x08 0x0008 1a 02 01 06 03 03 aa fe 12
16 aa fe 10 00 01 72 61 73 70 62 65 72 72 79 70 69 01 00 00 00 00
00
```

This will initiate advertisements on our Raspberry Pi Beacon.

To read more about `hcitool`, visit `https://linux.die.net/man/1/hcitool`.

You must be wondering what does this random string on numbers is advertising? The following table explains this in a lucid format:

Message bytes	Explanation/details
0x08	#OGF = Operation Group Field = Bluetooth Command Group = 0x08
0x0008	#OCF = Operation Command Field = HCI_LE_Set_Advertising_Data = 0x0008
1a	Length; the hexadecimal 17 converts to 26 decimal, which is the number of bytes that follow
02	Length
01	Flags data type value
06	Flags data
03	Length
03	Complete list of 16-bit Service UUIDs data type value
aa	16-bit Eddystone UUID

fe	16-bit Eddystone UUID
12	Length, which is the number of bytes that follow
16	Service Data type value
aa	16-bit Eddystone UUID
fe	16-bit Eddystone UUID
10	Frame Type = URL
00	TX Power (this should be calibrated)
01	URL Scheme (https://www. = 0x01)(http:// = 0x02)(https:// = 0x03).
72	'r' in hexadecimal
61	'a' in hexadecimal
73	's' in hexadecimal
70	'p' in hexadecimal
62	'b' in hexadecimal
65	'e' in hexadecimal
72	'r' in hexadecimal
72	'r' in hexadecimal
79	'y' in hexadecimal
70	'p' in hexadecimal
69	'i' in hexadecimal
01	.org (.org = 0x01)
00	
00	
00	
00	
00	

Please note that as of the writing of this, Eddystone offers a limited packet size of 31 bytes which places a limit on the complexity of URL(s) that can be broadcasted with it. Hence, if we need to broadcast complex URL(s), then we should make use of a URL shortening service. However, with the new standards introduced by Bluetooth 5, this limitation is anticipated to soon disappear.

The Beacon format must make some sense to you now.

 To read more detailed Eddystone-URL format, visit `https://github.com/google/eddystone/tree/master/eddystone-url`.

Generating the Beacon format for each URL can be little tedious hence there is already a nice tool available for that.

 To see the Eddystone-URL generating tool in action, visit `http://yencarnacion.github.io/eddystone-url-calculator/`.

Our Beacon is now continuously broadcasting the URL `www.raspberrypi.org`; we shall now write an app to detect that URL.

Writing an App to Detect the Beacon

Our Beacon is already up and advertising. We will now write an app to detect the Beacon and the contents of the advertisement. Although Eddystone has excellent documentation provided by Google for both Android and iOS. Eddystone is originally developed by Google and in general sense has a more elaborative setup on Android. Hence, we shall start with Android first and then move on to iOS. For iOS, we shall give you a head start on the code and then expect that you do the rest as an exercise to gain a solid footing.

Prerequisites for this section:

- A Raspberry Pi 3(setup as described in the previous section)

Android:

- Latest Android Studio
- A Latest Android Device(Preferable Samsung Galaxy S8, since it has support for Bluetooth 5 otherwise Any Device with an API Level of 23(Android M) is fine)
- Basic familiarity with Java and Android

iOS:

- XCode 8.2
- A latest iOS device(Our development device uses iOS 9.3.5)
- Basic familiarity with Swift 2.3 and iOS

Android

An interesting thing to note in our Android app is that our app would be making use of open source software developed by Google, which makes our life easier by parsing Eddystone advertisement data. We begin by creating an empty project in the Android Studio by the name of `AndroidBeaconScanner`. We have already done the project creation multiple times and hence we won't be repeating that here.

 During the project creation, choose the minimum API Level to be 21, since many of the API calls require minimum API Level to be 21.

Once we have finished creating our empty project, as a first step, we can define some simple user interface as follows:

1. We take a slightly different approach this time. After creating the project, rather initializing the UI as we did earlier, this time we go ahead and include(as described in step 2) the software which is provided *"as is"* by Google. The advantage of including this software in the very first step is that we won't be running into any build issues later on due to undefined classes.

2. We recommend creating a separate package for the software, which needs to be included as is. This can be done by navigating to **File** | **New** | **Package**, selecting **Package** and choosing a destination directory which is *Java* in our case. Please give your package a meaningful name. For simplicity, we just named ours as `google` as shown in the following screenshot:

Figure 13: Including software from Google

3. As shown in the preceding screenshot, we would need the following four files:
   - `BluetoothUuid.java`
   - `ScanRecord.java`
   - `EddystoneBeacon.java`
   - `UrlDevice.java`

These files are already hosted in Google's Physical Web repository.

Google's physical web repository is available here: `https://github.com/google/physical-web`.

We could have also included these files as a part of a bigger package/library, but we do not need everything else. Hence to slim it down, we shall include on only these four files. You can include these files by simply downloading those from GitHub and copying and pasting them in the *google* package. Please do remember the to change the *package name* statement at the very start(top of each file) with your own package name as shown in the preceding screenshot. We will explain the purpose of each of these files:

- `BluetoothUuid.java`: This contains standard service IDs as defined in Bluetooth assigned number documents. It also contains various methods to convert/parse bytes to UUID(s). It is used internally by `ScanRecord.java` to parse Service UUID(s).

 To know more about Bluetooth assigned numbers in **Service Discovery Protocol (SDP)**, visit `https://www.bluetooth.com/specifications/assigned-numbers/service-discovery`.

The `BluetoothUuid.java` file is hosted at Google's Physical Web repository on GitHub: `https://github.com/google/physical-web/blob/master/android/PhysicalWeb/app/src/main/java/org/physical_web/physicalweb/ble/BluetoothUuid.java`. Alternatively, you can also download it (plus the other three files) prebundled as a part of the current app we are building. The link for the app's code on Github, as always, is provided at the end of this section.

- `ScanRecord.java`: This represents scan records, containing `txPowerLevel`, `DeviceName`, and other relevant information discovered regarding BLE devices found during a BLE scan. The `ScanRecord.java` file at Google's Physical Web repository `https://github.com/google/physical-web/blob/master/android/PhysicalWeb/app/src/main/java/org/physical_web/physicalweb/ble/ScanRecord.java`.

- `EddystoneBeacon.java`: This represents the Eddystone advertisement format. It also contains methods to parse Eddystone advertisement data. The `EddystoneBeacon.java` file is available at Google's Physical Web repository `https://github.com/google/physical-web/blob/master/java/libs/src/main/java/org/physical_web/collection/EddystoneBeacon.java`.

In our app, we would be dealing specifically with Eddystone-URL packets.

To know more about Eddystone-URL packet format, visit `https://github.com/google/eddystone/tree/master/eddystone-url`.

- `UrlDevice.java`: This class represents any device, which can broadcast a URL. Since our beacon is advertising a URL, we will need this class to represent it. The `UrlDevice.java` file is available at Google's Physical Web repository `https://github.com/google/physical-web/blob/master/java/libs/src/main/java/org/physical_web/collection/UrlDevice.java`.

Application code

So far so good. At the end of previous step, we hope that you have included the earlier mentioned files in your code preferably in a separate package. Now, we start writing our App:

1. We shall create a simple UI, which is nothing much but just a text view on a screen to display our Beacon data. For this, navigate to the `activity_main.xml` file in the design view and drag and drop a **textView**. Apply constraints and position the text view to the top of the screen:

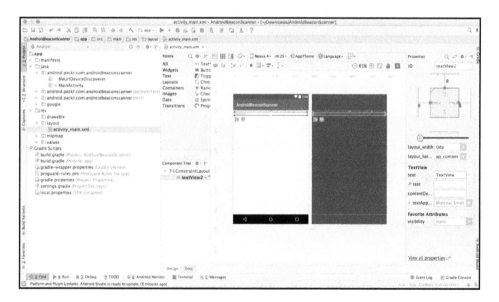

Figure 14: Adding the TextView

2. Our very basic UI is ready. Now, we need to scan and discover the Beacon first. For this, create a class by the name of `BleUrlDeviceDiscoverer` and make sure it implements `BluetoothAdapter.LeScanCallback`:

```
class BleUrlDeviceDiscoverer implements
BluetoothAdapter.LeScanCallback
```

3. We will now create the following interface and variable & and those to the `BleUrlDeviceDiscoverer` class as members:

```
public interface DeviceReporter {
  void reportUrlDevice(UrlDevice device);
  }

private DeviceReporter reporter;
```

This interface will ensure that whenever the Beacon is discovered, our UI (activity) is informed about it.

4. Also, please add the following member variables to the `BleUrlDeviceDiscoverer` class:

```
private static final String TAG =
  BleUrlDeviceDiscoverer.class.getSimpleName();
private static final ParcelUuid URIBEACON_SERVICE_UUID
  =ParcelUuid.fromString("0000FED8-0000-1000-8000-00805F9B34FB");
private static final ParcelUuid EDDYSTONE_URL_SERVICE_UUID
  =ParcelUuid.fromString("0000FEAA-0000-1000-8000-00805F9B34FB");
private BluetoothAdapter mBluetoothAdapter;
private Parcelable[] mScanFilterUuids;
private Context mContext;
private long mScanStartTime;
```

Before Eddystone, Google was working on URI Beacon format and later this format evolved as Eddystone. We will include the service ID(s) for both UriBeacon and Eddystone.

 To learn more about UriBeacon, visit `https://github.com/google/uribeacon`.

For Bluetooth interactions (initiating a scan), we declare a `BluetoothAdapter`. We also define an array of scan filters based on which we can filter specific service ID(s).

5. Please declare the following keys in the `BleUrlDeviceDiscoverer` class; these would be needed in creating the Beacon object once it is detected:

```
private static final String SCANTIME_KEY = "scantime";
private static final String TYPE_KEY = "type";
private static final String PUBLIC_KEY = "public";
private static final String TITLE_KEY = "title";
private static final String DESCRIPTION_KEY = "description";
private static final String RSSI_KEY = "rssi";
private static final String TXPOWER_KEY = "tx";
```

6. Our member variables are declared; now we shall go ahead and declare a constructor, which shall initialize some of our member variables, which we declared in the earlier steps.

```
public BleUrlDeviceDiscoverer(MainActivity mainActivity) {
  mContext = mainActivity;
  reporter = mainActivity;
  final BluetoothManager bluetoothManager = (BluetoothManager)
mContext.getSystemService(
  Context.BLUETOOTH_SERVICE);
  mBluetoothAdapter = bluetoothManager.getAdapter();
  mScanFilterUuids = new ParcelUuid[]{EDDYSTONE_URL_SERVICE_UUID};
  }
```

The constructor takes in the UI component (`mainActivity`) and initializes the context and the reporting interface variable so that it can form the UI as soon as the beacon is discovered. We use the context to initialize `bluetoothManager` from which we initialize the adapter.

 One thing we have deliberately left out of the App is to ask for Bluetooth and Location permissions regarding usability. We have done this many times in the past chapters. Do try to add them yourself. However, these permissions are essentially critical as, without these permissions, the app will not function at all.

We also initialize our scan filters so as to filter out Eddystone Beacons only.

7. We shall also need methods to start and stop BLE scanning. Define them as outlined here:

```
public synchronized void startScanImpl() {
 mScanStartTime = SystemClock.elapsedRealtime();
 mBluetoothAdapter.startLeScan(this);
}

public synchronized void stopScanImpl() {
 mBluetoothAdapter.stopLeScan(this);
}
```

8. As our BLE scan progresses, it shall report *all* the devices found. However, we are only interested in Eddystone Beacons, hence we will need to put a filtering mechanism in place:

```
private boolean leScanMatches(ScanRecord scanRecord) {
  if (mScanFilterUuids == null) {
    return true;
  }
  List services = scanRecord.getServiceUuids();
  if (services != null) {
    for (Parcelable uuid : mScanFilterUuids) {
      if (services.contains(uuid)) {
        return true;
      }
    }
  }
  return false;
}
```

In the preceding method, using the scan filters we initialized in the constructor to include only Eddystone Service UUID, we shall match each scanRecord to see whether it belongs to Eddystone service or not.

9. Now comes one of the most crucial parts, that is, receiving scan records. Once the scan is initiated, each BLE device found shall be delivered as a parameter to the method as shown in the following code block:

```
@Override
public void onLeScan(final BluetoothDevice device, final int rssi,
final byte[] scanBytes) {
 ScanRecord scanRecord = ScanRecord.parseFromBytes(scanBytes);
 if (!leScanMatches(scanRecord)) {
 return;
 }
```

```
 byte[] urlServiceData =
scanRecord.getServiceData(EDDYSTONE_URL_SERVICE_UUID);
 byte[] uriServiceData =
scanRecord.getServiceData(URIBEACON_SERVICE_UUID);
 EddystoneBeacon beacon =
EddystoneBeacon.parseFromServiceData(urlServiceData,
uriServiceData);
 if (beacon == null) {
 return;
 }
 UrlDevice urlDevice = null;
 try {
 urlDevice = createUrlDeviceBuilder(TAG + device.getAddress() +
beacon.getUrl(),
 beacon.getUrl())
 .setRssi(rssi)
 .setTxPower(beacon.getTxPowerLevel())
 .setDeviceType("ble")
 .build();
 } catch (JSONException e) {
 e.printStackTrace();
 }
 reporter.reportUrlDevice(urlDevice);
}
```

In the preceding method, we convert the data received from the scan to a scan record and we use our filtering mechanism, which we defined in the previous step to find scanned records, which are specific to Eddystone advertisements only. Once the matching scan record is found, we try to convert that data to a EddyStone Beacon using the software from Google, which we included earlier. Once we have a valid Eddystone-URL beacon object, we then finally convert it to a `UrlDevice` and pass to the UI (`mainActivity`). The only missing piece now is the `URLDeviceBuilder`, which we shall define in the next step.

10. We now define a method to convert beacon data to a `UrlDevice` object. For this, define the following method in the `BleUrlDeviceDiscoverer` class:

```
protected UrlDeviceBuilder createUrlDeviceBuilder(String id, String
url) throws JSONException {
        return new UrlDeviceBuilder(id, url)
                .setScanTimeMillis(SystemClock.elapsedRealtime() -
mScanStartTime);
    }
```

11. We shall also need to define a `UrlDeviceBuilder` class, which takes in the ID and the URL being broadcasted by the Beacon and constructs a `UrlDevice` object from it:

```
static class UrlDeviceBuilder extends UrlDevice.Builder {

/**
 * Constructor for the UrlDeviceBuilder.
 * @param id The id of the UrlDevice.
 * @param url The url of the UrlDevice.
 */
public UrlDeviceBuilder(String id, String url) {
super(id, url);
}

/**
 * Set the device type.
 * @return The builder with type set.
 */
 public UrlDeviceBuilder setDeviceType(String type) throws
JSONException {
addExtra(TYPE_KEY, type);
return this;
}

/**
 * Setter for the ScanTimeMillis.
 * @param timeMillis The scan time of the UrlDevice.
 * @return The builder with ScanTimeMillis set.
 */
 public UrlDeviceBuilder setScanTimeMillis(long timeMillis) throws
JSONException {
addExtra(SCANTIME_KEY, timeMillis);
return this;
}

/**
```

```
 * Set the public key to false.
 * @return The builder with public set to false.
 */
public UrlDeviceBuilder setPrivate() throws JSONException {
addExtra(PUBLIC_KEY, false);
return this;
}

/**
 * Set the public key to true.
 * @return The builder with public set to true.
 */
public UrlDeviceBuilder setPublic() throws JSONException {
addExtra(PUBLIC_KEY, true);
return this;
}

/**
 * Set the title.
 * @param title corresonding to UrlDevice.
 * @return The builder with title
 */
public UrlDeviceBuilder setTitle(String title) throws
JSONException {
addExtra(TITLE_KEY, title);
return this;
}

/**
 * Set the description.
 * @param description corresonding to UrlDevice.
 * @return The builder with description
 */
public UrlDeviceBuilder setDescription(String description) throws
JSONException {
addExtra(DESCRIPTION_KEY, description);
return this;
}

/**
 * Setter for the RSSI.
 * @param rssi The RSSI of the UrlDevice.
 * @return The builder with RSSI set.
 */
public UrlDeviceBuilder setRssi(int rssi) throws JSONException {
addExtra(RSSI_KEY, rssi);
return this;
}
```

```
/**
 * Setter for the TX power.
 * @param txPower The TX power of the UrlDevice.
 * @return The builder with TX power set.
 */
public UrlDeviceBuilder setTxPower(int txPower) throws
JSONException {
addExtra(TXPOWER_KEY, txPower);
return this;
}
}
```

Define the preceding static class inside the `BleUrlDeviceDiscoverer` class. This class contains various setter methods to set key parameters and build a `UrlDevice` object from data received from the Eddystone-URL beacon using the `UrlDevice` class, which we included earlier as a part of the software from Google.

12. We are almost done with our setup. We now just need to hook up `BleUrlDeviceDiscoverer` to the UI (MainActivity). For this, implement the `DeviceReporter` interface in the `MainActivity`:

```
public class MainActivity extends AppCompatActivity implements
BleUrlDeviceDiscoverer.DeviceReporter
```

Also, proceed to implement the `report` method of the interface in the manner shown in the following code block:

```
@Override
public void reportUrlDevice(UrlDevice device) {
((TextView)findViewById(R.id.textView2)).setText(device.get
Url());
}
```

The last missing piece is to initialize the `BleUrlDeviceDiscoverer` in the `onCreate` method and start the scan as soon as the app is started:

```
@Override
 protected void onCreate(Bundle savedInstanceState) {
 super.onCreate(savedInstanceState);
 setContentView(R.layout.activity_main);

 BleUrlDeviceDiscoverer deviceDiscoverer = new
 BleUrlDeviceDiscoverer(this);
 deviceDiscoverer.startScanImpl();
 }
```

And Voila! As soon as you start the app,

Please note that you will need a physical device to test the Android Sample. If you are already familiar with Android then it should be as simple as connecting the device via USB to the development computer and pressing the "Run" button. If you run into some issues, then please refer to this link: `https://developer.android.com/training/basics/firstapp/running-app.html`

And if the Raspberry Pi beacon is broadcasting, you should be able to see the broadcasted URL being populated in the textview.

Figure 15: Beacon Broadcast Detection

An important troubleshooting tip is as follows:

 Please note again that it is important that you enable the permissions for Bluetooth and Location, otherwise you will not see anything and may end up spending some precious time debugging it.

We are done with the Android app. All of the code that we went over in this section is available at the link mentioned next.

 Find the code for the `AndroidBeaconScanner` app at `https://github.com/madhurbhargava/AndroidBeaconScanner`.

iOS

We hope that you have already gained some solid footing on the Eddystone-URL advertisement format. For iOS, Google has already provided a very simple and clearly defined Beacon Scanner Sample app, which shall work out of the box for our Raspberry Pi Beacon.

 To download the code for the iOS Eddystone Beacon Scanner Sample from Google (in Swift), navigate to `https://github.com/madhurbhargava/eddystone/tree/master/tools/ios-eddystone-scanner-sample/EddystoneScannerSampleSwift`.

If you run the app, you would be able to see the Beacon URL being printed in the logs. We do not intend to reinvent the wheel and would urge you to go ahead and download the code from the link mentioned and figure out what it is doing.

We shall brush over some key points to give you a quick start in the iOS Sample (Swift):

1. The Swift iOS Beacon Scanner Sample code contains the following two important classes:

    1. `BeaconScanner.swift`: This handles Beacon scanning and data parsing.
    2. `Eddystone.swift`: This converts the raw Beacon data to Eddystone Beacon object.

2. We shall only focus on the `BeaconScanner` class since the `Eddystone` class is pretty similar to the one we saw in the preceding Android sample. The `ViewController` class creates a `beaconScanner` object and calls the `startScanning` method on the `beaconScanner` object as shown next:

```
override func viewDidLoad() {
    super.viewDidLoad()
    self.beaconScanner = BeaconScanner()
    self.beaconScanner!.delegate = self
    self.beaconScanner!.startScanning()
}
```

You can find the preceding code in the `ViewController` class included in the Swift sample. You can easily compare this to what we do in the `onCreate` method of the `MainActivity` file in the Android Sample since this is very much similar.

3. Post initialization, the `BeaconScanner` class initiates the search for Eddystone Beacons once the Central Manager (Bluetooth Adapter) is powered on, which it does via the following piece of code:

```
private func startScanningSynchronized() {
    if self.centralManager.state != .PoweredOn {
       NSLog("CentralManager state is %d, cannot start scan",
self.centralManager.state.rawValue)
       self.shouldBeScanning = true
    } else {
       NSLog("Starting to scan for Eddystones")
       let services = [CBUUID(string: "FEAA")]
       let options =
[CBCentralManagerScanOptionAllowDuplicatesKey : true]
self.centralManager.scanForPeripheralsWithServices(services,
options: options)
    }
}
```

You can find the preceding code in the `BeaconScanner` class.

4. Once a Eddystone is found, `BeaconScanner` tries to parse the data associated with the Beacon and this happens in the method mentioned next:

```
func centralManager(central: CBCentralManager,
didDiscoverPeripheral peripheral: CBPeripheral,
advertisementData: [String : AnyObject], RSSI: NSNumber)
```

We are afraid that we will be spoiling all the fun for you if we go any further than this, and would request that you go over the code yourself as an exercise to understand what happens after this.

> The iOS code is not that very different from the Android code. It basically does the same thing—it searches for the Beacons by navigating to **Eddystone service** | **Beacon Found** | **Parses Data** | **Logs DataSummary**.

The preceding exercise would not only give you a solid footing, but will also help to make clear that with Android or iOS, whatever may be the platform, the underlying technology (Bluetooth Low Energy) remains the same. The medium of expression (Java versus Swift) might differ a little bit, but the underlying implementations are inherently similar.

Summary

Beacons are a different and an important paradigm related to Bluetooth Low Energy. They are becoming increasingly popular day by day. Google and Apple already foresaw that, and defined their own standard formats for Beacon advertisements which we covered in this chapter. We also briefly discussed Physical Web, which is Google's grand plan to convert *Internet of things* to *Internet of* everything. We shall discuss Physical Web in detail in the last chapter.

As this chapter draws to a conclusion, we move on to the grand finale, our final project for this book, where we design an industrial solution for warehouse monitoring. We shall also introduce a new interesting sensor in that chapter. The project is of utmost importance, given the fact that that it is already being applied in warehouses across the US and UK. So, stay tuned!

6

Weather Monitoring Using BLE in Warehouses

Creativity is just connecting things.

- Steve Jobs

In this chapter, we shall build a warehouse monitoring system, which is an Industrial grade solution and will help us in better understanding the roots of the foundations of IoT based on Bluetooth Low Energy via the following topics:

- Problem Statement and Solution Design
- Temperature and Humidity Sensors
- Designing the Monitoring App
- Practical Applications

Through the earlier mentioned topics, on a very high level, we shall attempt to understand why there is a need for such a solution, eventually translating that need into a problem statement and finally attempting to address the problem statement by proposing a solution design. This chapter will also introduce you to a real-life scenario, which can be addressed by a solution designed around IoT and BLE. Apart from solution design, it will also augment your pre-existing skill set from the previous chapters by adding the knowledge of some more sensors to it.

In the next section, we shall begin our system design process by understanding the problem at hand and its solution design. Since the sensors will play a key role in the design of the solution, we shall then move on to discussing them after we have understood the problem.

Problem Statement and Solution Design

While designing any system, it is imperative to understand the following:

- Which problem does the system address?
- How do the various individual parts in the system communicate with each other or how does the flow of data take place in the system?

Not to bog you down with the details, we shall only elaborate on the essential parts and design the bare minimum system so that you can get an idea of data flow and overall system design. Let's understand the problem at hand first, by eventually coming up with a problem statement.

Apart from several other items, warehouses are also used for storing vegetables, food, and medicines. Specifically for these items, it is crucial to maintain a correct balance of the temperature and humidity; otherwise, there is a risk of major losses. Hence, a warehouse deploys specially designed monitoring systems, which continuously monitor the climate inside a warehouse. If anything goes awry, then these systems are capable of raising alarms as well as indicating it to the remote monitoring team. The remote monitoring team can immediately summon on site and put a cap on the situation at hand.

These remote monitoring systems work through an intelligent network of sensors, connected to remote backend for monitoring and notifications. Our system design will follow a similar approach as shown in the following diagram:

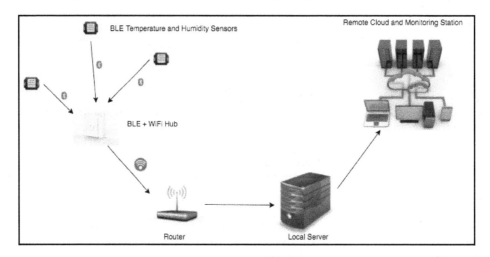

Figure 1: System design

To solve the problem stated earlier, one of the solutions is to strategically plant **BLE Temperature and Humidity Sensors** across the warehouse, which can then record the climate data and keep sending it to a central hub device, which is capable of communicating over both **BLE + WiFi Hub**. The **WiFi Hub** is then responsible for connecting to a local **Router**, which can finally enable the data upload to the **Remote Cloud and Monitoring Station** periodically.

 The data flow in the preceding system is again based on the one way/simplex communication similar to the one in case of Beacons as elaborated in the previous chapter.

With the periodic data now at their hands, the remote monitoring team can efficiently monitor them and can make crucial decisions on the fly. This design even enables large warehouses to operate on a skeletal crew of 1-2 personnel.

Just try to imagine, what would it take to monitor the various crucial climatic parameters, if this or a similar solution was not in place.

Temperature and Humidity Sensors

There are already temperature and humidity sensors commercially available in the market for both industrial and home solutions.

 You will find numerous climatic sensor solutions on the internet. For example, ONSET is one such company providing *Temperature and Relative Humidity Data Loggers & Sensors*. To know about it, visit `http://www.onsetcomp.com/products/data-loggers-sensors/temperature-relative-humidity-rh`.

One of the advantages about choosing a complete sensor solution rather than individual and standalone sensors is that sensor-based solutions are well packaged and come with extensive documentation and support. For example, the following is a *TEMPERATURE-HUMIDITY SENSOR + EXTRAS* known as *DHT22*:

Figure 2: DHT22 Temperature and humidity sensor; source: `www.adafruit.com`

This is a low cost and basic temperature and humidity sensor, which is great for learning about sensors and their internals. However, if you are looking forward to building a complete sensor-oriented solution, then this might not be the best choice since you may want something that you could use just out of the box and hence focus on the complete solution rather than getting into the nitty-gritties of the sensor setup.

To know more about *DHT22,* visit `http://www.waveshare.com/wiki/DHT22_Temperature-Humidity_Sensor.`

Even if you are creating a small demo/prototype project, before you can read data from DHT22, you will still need to at least provide it a basic housing for practical usage/protection and connect it to a power supply. On the other hand, sensor solutions offered by companies such as ONSET come completely packaged, ready to be used, as shown below:

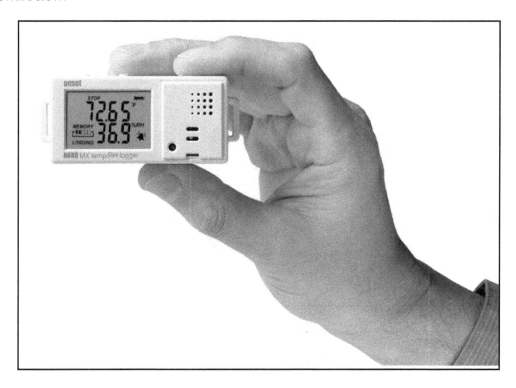

Figure 3: A neatly packaged sensor solution; source: www.onsetcomp.com

You can just unbox the solution, insert a battery, plant it at the place where it is needed, and you are good to go.

To read more about the sensor solution shown in preceding image, visit http://www.onsetcomp.com/products/data-loggers/mx1101.

We hope that the preceding explanation might have given you an insight into the difference between an individual sensor and a sensor solution.

For the purpose of creating our warehouse monitoring solution, we would be using one such sensor solution or rather a sensor kit, as this would make your life much easier. Since you can then just go on to write the app and make the data available online, which would be the ideal scenario if you ever decide to implement this solution in a real warehouse. Hence, allow me to present the CC2650STK, which includes 10 low-power, tiny MEMS sensors:

Figure 4: CC2650STK SensorTag Kit; source: e2e.ti.com

Also popularly known as the SensorTag IoT Kit, this sensor solution offered by Texas Instruments is even smaller than a credit card and operates on a single coin cell battery that contains 10 onboard sensors, which support the following:

1. Light
2. Digital microphone
3. Magnetic sensor
4. Humidity
5. Pressure
6. Accelerometer
7. Gyroscope
8. Magnetometer
9. Object temperature
10. Ambient temperature

As you can already notice that this kit can sense a lot more than just humidity and temperature, which makes the eventual possibilities with this kit to be boundless and since it is a sensor solution, hence it can be used right out of the box.

 For the specifications of CC2650STK, visit: `http://www.ti.com/tool/cc2650stk#1`.

Rather than bogging you down with the specifications of CC2650STK, it would be better if we interrogate the SensorTag itself with the App that we wrote in `Chapter 3`, *Building a Service Explorer App*, so that we could identify what the sensor has to offer.

Interrogating Temperature and Humidity Sensors

Consider yourself to be a smart engineer working for a company which provides warehousing and cold storage solutions and as a next step wants to efficiently monitor the climatic conditions, specifically temperature and humidity in each of its warehouses/storage houses:

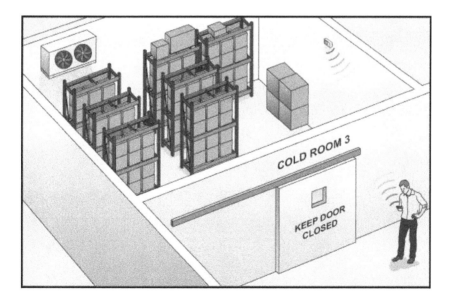

Figure 5: Efficient monitoring temperatures in cold storages; source: `http://www.onsetcomp.com/`

However, before moving on to implement the full-fledged solution at a global scale, the CTO of the company has personally asked you to design a small demo/prototype as a proof of concept based on CC2650STK sensor kit for demonstration purposes to the board so as to convince the board members and also to secure the funds for the global operation.

Since our demo/prototype heavily relies on the communication with CC2650STK and hence we would be tackling that first. The exercise that we are going to do will help us in knowing the SensorTag better. Once we know the individual services and characteristics present on the SensorTag, it would become very easy to interact with the SensorTag kit to read the temperature and humidity values.

Following are the pre-requisites for this section:

Android:

- Latest Android Studio
- A Latest Android Device (Preferable Samsung Galaxy S8, since it has support for Bluetooth 5; otherwise Any Device with an API Level of 23(Android M) is fine)
- Android Application Code from `Chapter 3`, *Building a Service Explorer App*

Hardware:

- Texas Instruments CC2650 STK SensorTag

Let's get started by eating our own dog food.

1. After making sure the battery is in place, Turn on the SensorTag using the power button (as shown in the following figure) in the advertising mode:

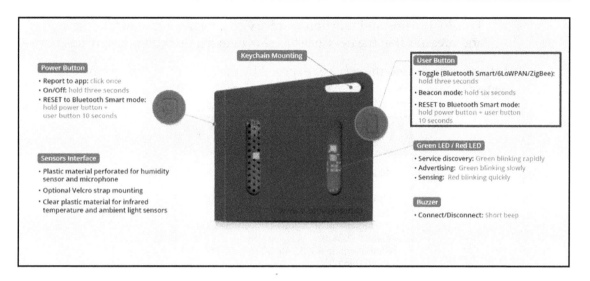

Figure 6: Sensor tag operation details: source: e2e.ti.com

2. Now, run the AndroidBLEServiceExplorer app using Android Studio, which we wrote as part of Chapter 3, *Building a Service Explorer App* on the Android device and use it to scan the nearby BLE devices. If the SensorTag was switched on successfully, then it would show up on the list of discovered devices as shown in the following screenshot:

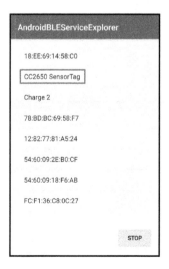

Figure 7: Discovering CC2650 SensorTag

True to its name and function, our Service Explorer app finds the SensorTag and presents it in the device list as shown in the preceding screenshot.

3. Let's now try to find the services exposed by the SensorTag. Tap on the CC2650 SensorTag list item to initiate service discovery:

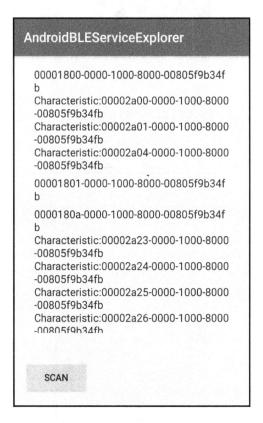

Figure 8: Service discovery on SensorTag

If all goes well, then you should be greeted with a long list of services and characteristics as shown in the preceding screenshot.

4. The SensorTag exposes the following services:

Service UUID(s)	Service names
00001800-0000-1000-8000-00805f9b34fb	Generic Access Service
00001801-0000-1000-8000-00805f9b34fb	Generic Attribute Service
0000180a-0000-1000-8000-00805f9b34fb	Device Information Service
0000180f-0000-1000-8000-00805f9b34fb	Battery Service
f000aa00-0451-4000-b000-000000000000	*IR Temperature Service*
f000aa20-0451-4000-b000-000000000000	*Humidity Service*
f000aa40-0451-4000-b000-000000000000	Barometer Service
f000aa80-0451-4000-b000-000000000000	Movement Service
f000aa70-0451-4000-b000-000000000000	Luxometer Service
0000ffe0-0000-1000-8000-00805f9b34fb	Simple Keys Service
f000aa64-0451-4000-b000-000000000000	I/O Service
f000ac00-0451-4000-b000-000000000000	Register Service
f000ccc0-0451-4000-b000-000000000000	Connection Control Service
f000ffc0-0451-4000-b000-000000000000	Over the Air Download (OAD) Service

Curious about how we found out which UUID(s) belonged to which services? As we already mentioned previously, one of the advantages of using a sensor solution/sensor kit as compared to an individual sensor is the bundled documentation/support that comes with it.

 To know more about the services exposed by the SensorTag and their characteristics, refer to http://e2e.ti.com/cfs-file/__key/
communityserver-discussions-components-files/538/attr_5F00_
cc2650-sensortag.html.

For the task at hand, we are interested in the temperature and the Humidity Service, although we do advise that you go through various other sensor parameters that the SensorTag has to offer.

5. Once we have identified the services that we are interested in, it is worthwhile to have a look at the characteristics that they have to offer. As per our BLE Service Explorer app, the temperature service offers the following characteristics:

UUID	Name	Functionality
0xAA01	IR Temperature Data	Temperature related data
0xAA02	IR Temperature Config	Configuration/Control for the temperature sensor
0xAA03	IR Temperature Period	Temperature period

Humidity Service offers the following characteristics:

UUID	Name	Functionality
0xAA21	Humidity Data	Humidity related data
0xAA22	Humidity Config	Configuration/Control for the humidity sensor
0xAA23	Humidity Period	Humidity period

For the details of services and characteristics offered by SensorTag, visit `http://processors.wiki.ti.com/images/a/a8/BLE_SensorTag_GATT_Server.pdf`.

Looks like we know enough about the SensorTag now to start building our warehouse monitoring app to demonstrate the feasibility of the prototype to the CTO and the company board members.

Designing the Monitoring App

The basic idea behind our setup is based on the system design we described in the Solution Design section previously. Our app behaves as the BLE + Wi-Fi Hub, reading data directly from the sensors planted on store/warehouse shelves and uploads it to the backend (Firebase) for monitoring purposes.

A Note - We would be implementing a lot of functionality in this section. Please don't let that scare you. As a visual aid to give you a better understanding of the code that you would be implementing in this section, we have added a flowchart which outlines the flow of our App, towards the end of this section. Once you have implemented the code, we request you to review your code with the flowchart serving as a guidance tool. This will give you a much better understanding of the overall functionality of the App.

Following are the pre-requisites for this section,

Android:

- Latest Android Studio
- A Latest Android Device (Preferable Samsung Galaxy S8, since it has support for Bluetooth 5; otherwise Any Device with an API Level of 23(Android M) is fine)
- Basic familiarity with Java and Android

iOS:

- XCode 8.2
- A latest iOS device (Our development device uses iOS 9.3.5)
- Basic familiarity with Swift 2.3 and iOS

Hardware:

- Texas Instruments CC2650 STK SensorTag

We request you to please do the following steps on a Mac based environment since then it would be possible to execute the steps for both Android and iOS on a single development environment.

Let's get started.

Android

We begin by creating an empty project by the name of `AndroidWarehouseMonitor`.

1. We begin by defining the user interface to display the current temperature and humidity values on the screen. To do this, we define our UI by updating the `activity_main.xml` file. Remove whatever code is present in this file and you can either add the following code directly to the `activity_main.xml` file or add the UI via the UI editor:

```xml
<?xml version="1.0" encoding="utf-8"?>
<android.support.constraint.ConstraintLayout
xmlns:android="http://schemas.android.com/apk/res/android"
 xmlns:app="http://schemas.android.com/apk/res-auto"
 xmlns:tools="http://schemas.android.com/tools"
 android:layout_width="match_parent"
 android:layout_height="match_parent"
tools:context="android.packt.com.androidwarehousemonitor.MainAc
tivity">
<TextView
 android:id="@+id/textView"
 android:layout_width="0dp"
 android:layout_height="217dp"
 android:layout_marginEnd="8dp"
 android:layout_marginLeft="8dp"
 android:layout_marginRight="8dp"
 android:layout_marginStart="8dp"
 android:layout_marginTop="8dp"
 android:text="Temperature:"
 android:textAppearance="@style/TextAppearance.AppCompat.Large"
 app:layout_constraintHorizontal_bias="0.526"
 app:layout_constraintLeft_toLeftOf="parent"
 app:layout_constraintRight_toRightOf="parent"
 app:layout_constraintTop_toTopOf="parent" />
<TextView
 android:id="@+id/textView2"
 android:layout_width="match_parent"
 android:layout_height="219dp"
 android:layout_marginBottom="8dp"
 android:layout_marginLeft="8dp"
 android:layout_marginRight="8dp"
 android:layout_marginTop="8dp"
 android:text="Humidity:"
 android:textAppearance="@style/TextAppearance.AppCompat.Large"
 app:layout_constraintBottom_toBottomOf="parent"
 app:layout_constraintLeft_toLeftOf="parent"
 app:layout_constraintRight_toRightOf="parent"
```

```
app:layout_constraintTop_toBottomOf="@+id/textView" />
</android.support.constraint.ConstraintLayout>
```

Addition of the preceding code should result in the following UI:

Figure 9: Temperature and humidity data UI for Android warehouse monitor

If you run the app now and are able to see the preceding UI, then congratulations, we just completed the simple UI layer of our app.

2. With our UI being ready, we shall now move on to add the code, which interacts with the sensor. However, before moving on to the sensor interaction code, we would like to let you in on a little secret. If you remember from the previous chapters, we did show a dialog to remind the user that he/she needs to switch on the location permissions manually by navigating to **Settings**. However, we have not entirely been honest with you in this case (and that is of course to keep it simple in the start). Since this can also be done from the app itself and hence, in this example we shall demonstrate the same. For this, add the following `ensureLocationPermissionIsEnabled` method to the `MainActivity` class:

```
private void ensureLocationPermissionIsEnabled() {
  if (Build.VERSION.SDK_INT >= 23 &&
ContextCompat.checkSelfPermission(this,
```

```
android.Manifest.permission.ACCESS_COARSE_LOCATION) !=
PackageManager.PERMISSION_GRANTED) {
 ActivityCompat.requestPermissions(this, new String[]{
  android.Manifest.permission.ACCESS_COARSE_LOCATION},
REQUEST_LOCATION);
 return;
 }
 }
```

After adding the preceding code and compiling the project, you will get an error regarding REQUEST_LOCATION not being found. For that error to go away, add the following member variable to the MainActivity class:

```
private static final int REQUEST_LOCATION = 1;
```

After adding the ensureLocationPermissionIsEnabled method to our code, we no longer need to create a custom dialog to remind the user to navigate to **Settings** and switch on the permissions for the location manually. The preceding method checks whether the location permission is granted, and if not, then it requests the permission from the system.

 Note that Android Marshmallow (API Level 23) introduced the runtime permission model, which allows the apps to request user permissions in Android at runtime, rather than at compile time, which is also the reason why we check for API Level in the preceding code before requesting runtime permissions. To read more about runtime permission model, visit https://developer.android.com/training/permissions/requesting. html.

The preceding method uses the ActivityCompat class, which does all the hard work for us all in a single line of code.

3. The ActivityCompat class also provides the callback method, which gets called with user's selection result (whether or not the user granted the permission). Depending on the result, we can take appropriate action. We shall also implement this callback method, which is called onRequestPermissionResult, to listen for results of the permission request presented to the user. Add the following method to your MainActivity class:

```
@Override
public void onRequestPermissionsResult(int requestCode,
                                     String permissions[],
    int[] grantResults) {
      switch (requestCode) {
        case REQUEST_LOCATION: {
```

```
                // If request is cancelled, the result arrays are
empty.
                if (grantResults.length > 0
                        && grantResults[0] ==
PackageManager.PERMISSION_GRANTED) {
                    Log.i(TAG, "Permission Granted");
                } else {
                    Toast.makeText(getApplicationContext(),
                        "Location Permission Not granted",
Toast.LENGTH_LONG).show();
                    finish();
                }
                break;
            }
            default:
        }
    }
```

The preceding method simply logs it to the console if the permission has been granted; otherwise, it finishes the activity and exits the app. We have added the necessary methods, now we need to call them too.

4. For calling the methods that we added earlier in *Step 2* regarding enabling of location permissions, we shall add a checkPermissions method to our MainActivity class:

```
private void checkPermissions(BluetoothAdapter
bluetoothAdapter) {
  if (!bluetoothAdapter.isEnabled()) {
  Intent enableBtIntent = new
Intent(BluetoothAdapter.ACTION_REQUEST_ENABLE);
  startActivityForResult(enableBtIntent, REQUEST_ENABLE_BT);
  return;
  }
  ensureLocationPermissionIsEnabled();
  }
```

For the code to compile successfully, define the following member variable in the MainActivity class:

```
private static final int REQUEST_ENABLE_BT = 0;
```

The earlier mentioned checkPermissions method will be responsible for enabling Bluetooth and location permissions.

5. In the previous step, we start the **System Default** setting activity for the user and let the user decide whether he/she does or does not want to switch the Bluetooth on. However, we are interested to know user's decision, for which we override the following method `onActivityResult` to the `MainActivity` class:

```
@Override
protected void onActivityResult(int requestCode, int
resultCode, Intent data) {
  if (requestCode == REQUEST_ENABLE_BT && resultCode == -1) {
   ensureLocationPermissionIsEnabled();
   return;
  }
  Toast.makeText(this, "Bluetooth not turned on",
Toast.LENGTH_LONG).show();
   finish();
  }
```

The result of user's choice (whether the user decided to turn on the Bluetooth or not), will be returned in this method. Note that this is once again a slightly different approach than we have used in the earlier code samples where the app used to turn on the Bluetooth itself rather than navigating the user to settings. Also, we are being a little more strict here since we directly finish the Activity if the user does not turn on the Bluetooth, since there isn't much left to do in that case.

6. Let's handle another case, which we have bypassed until now. Earlier we have never handled the case where a device might not have Bluetooth Support at all. Since we are going the whole nine yards in this chapter, we shall demonstrate that too. Update the `onResume` method to the one shown next:

```
@Override
    protected void onResume() {
        super.onResume();
        BluetoothManager btManager = (BluetoothManager)
getSystemService(BLUETOOTH_SERVICE);
        BluetoothAdapter btAdapter = btManager != null ?
btManager.getAdapter() : null;
        if (btAdapter == null) {
            Toast.makeText(getApplicationContext(),
                    "No Bluetooth Support found",
Toast.LENGTH_LONG).show();
            finish();
            return;
        }
        checkPermissions(btAdapter);
```

```
}
```

The onResume method in the MainActivity class, first performs a check whether there is Bluetooth Support available on the device itself and if not, it finishes the activity. However, if Bluetooth Support is found, then it checks for other permissions. This is one of the best key practices for Android. Given the fragmentation in the Android hardware market, it is very much possible that our app may be run on one of the devices which has no Bluetooth hardware at all. In the preceding code, we handle that situation too, which we overlooked in all of the previous code samples.

7. We are almost done with the implementation of our new way of requesting and handling Bluetooth and location permissions. However, do remember to add the necessary permissions--Access Coarse Location, Bluetooth, Bluetooth Admin, and internet to the Android Manifest, otherwise our app will not work as expected. If you are still confused about how to do this, then refer to step 6 under Android app code setup in Chapter 3, *Building a Service Explorer App.*

8. Our app assumes to be operated in a scenario where the SensorTag (attached to warehouse shelves) is up and advertising always and hence as soon as the App begins its operation, it tries to filter out the SensorTag from the list of broadcasting devices, connect to it and read temperature and Humidity Data continuously. We have already demonstrated the code for the scanning of Bluetooth Low energy devices in the earlier chapters. Add a method called startScanning to the MainActivity class. If you need help in the method definition, then please refer to steps 2 and 3 regarding *Bluetooth Initialization* under Android app code setup in Chapter 2, *Setting Up.* Note that you will not able to use the code of startScanning method as is, since we no longer have the same UI.

Apart from the UI elements, you will also need to declare and define-- BluetoothAdapter, BluetoothManager, BluetoothLeScanner and last but not the least ScanCallback for receiving the scan results in order to successfully implement the scan functionality.

Assuming that you have successfully implemented the `startScanning` method, we now need to call it from two places, firstly, immediately after the user grants the location permission. For this, add the method call to the `startScanning` method to the `onRequestPermissionResult` method(which we earlier implemented in *Step 3* above) as shown next:

```
if (grantResults.length > 0 && grantResults[0] ==
PackageManager.PERMISSION_GRANTED) {
  Log.i(TAG, "Permission Granted");
  startScanning();
}
```

And secondly, if you have already granted all the permissions during the initial run of the app, we also add the method call for the `startScanning` method to the `ensureLocationPermissionIsEnabled` method(which we earlier implemented in *Step 2* above) as shown next:

```
private void ensureLocationPermissionIsEnabled() {
    if (Build.VERSION.SDK_INT >= 23 &&
ContextCompat.checkSelfPermission(this,
android.Manifest.permission.ACCESS_COARSE_LOCATION) !=
PackageManager.PERMISSION_GRANTED) {
        ActivityCompat.requestPermissions(this, new
String[]{
android.Manifest.permission.ACCESS_COARSE_LOCATION},
REQUEST_LOCATION);
        return;
    }
    startScanning();
}
```

We have implemented our Device Scan code. Now, we need to define a callback which handles the devices found.

9. If you were able to accomplish the previous step successfully, then your implementation of `startScanning` method will be making use of a `ScanCallback`, where the results of the scan get delivered. Please define the `ScanCallback` in the `MainActivity` class as shown next:

```
// Device scan callback.
private ScanCallback leScanCallback = new ScanCallback() {
    @Override
    public void onScanResult(int callbackType, ScanResult
result) {
        if (result.getDevice() != null) {
            if (result.getDevice().getName() != null &&
```

```
result.getDevice().getName().contains(NAME_TAG)) {
                Log.i(TAG, result.getDevice().getName());
                if (connected == false) {
                    connected = true;
bluetoothLeScanner.stopScan(leScanCallback);
result.getDevice().connectGatt(MainActivity.this, true,
gattCallback);
                }
            }
        }
    }
};
```

Notice the preceding piece of code closely, which is filtering available devices on the basis of names of the devices found. The above mentioned piece of code uses a few variables, which need to be declared in the `MainActivity` class as shown below:

```
private static String NAME_TAG = "SensorTag";
private boolean connected = false;
```

We will need to match the name of each device found with the name of the `SensorTag` and the `NAME_TAG` variable will help us in exactly that. Once the correct match is found, we initiate a connection by calling the `connectGatt` method and indicate that the connection request has been made by updating the state of `connected` variable.

10. In the last step, the call to `connectGatt` method takes three arguments. The last argument is a `callback` method which can be used for:
    1. Monitoring connection state changes
    2. Service discovery
    3. Characteristic changes

    We will initially implement this callback in the `MainActivity` class for just listening to connection state changes as shown next:

```
protected BluetoothGattCallback gattCallback = new
BluetoothGattCallback() {
    @Override
    public void onConnectionStateChange(BluetoothGatt gatt,
int status, int newState) {
        super.onConnectionStateChange(gatt, status,
newState);
        if (newState == BluetoothGatt.STATE_CONNECTED) {
            Log.i(TAG, "onConnectionStateChange() -
```

```
                            STATE_CONNECTED");
                                    gatt.discoverServices();
                            }
                    }
            };
```

As per the preceding implementation, if the connection succeeds, then we initiate service discovery.

11. We are interested in two services namely, `IR_TEMPERATURE_SERVICE` and `HUMIDITY_SERVICE`, hence we first define their UUID(s) in the `MainActivity` class:

```
private static final String UUID_IR_TEMPERATURE_SERVICE =
"f000aa00-0451-4000-b000-000000000000";
private static final String UUID_HUMIDITY_SERVICE =
"f000aa20-0451-4000-b000-000000000000";
```

Note that although we would be defining the UUIDs for both `TEMPERATURE_SERVICE` and `HUMIDITY_SERVICE`, we would only be demonstrating reading data from the `TEMPERATURE_SERVICE` in the Android code sample. Reading data from the `HUMIDITY_SERVICE` is very much similar and is left for you as an exercise. Hence, we shall focus specifically on the details of `TEMPERATURE_SERVICE` now onwards.

The `TEMPERATURE_SERVICE` on the SensorTag consists of two important characteristics, namely, the *Data Characteristic* and the *Configuration Characteristic*.

 Visit the following link to get insights regarding characteristics exposed by the SensorTag Temperature Service: `http://processors.wiki.ti.com/images/a/a8/BLE_SensorTag_GATT_Server.pdf`

As the name suggests, the data characteristic holds the temperature data and supports *reading* that data and *enabling/disabling Notifications* for the temperature data. We shall be interacting with both of these characteristics. Hence, define these in the `MainActivity` class as shown next:

```
//Characteristic UUIDs
private static final UUID
UUID_CHARACTERISTIC_TEMPERATURE_DATA =
UUID.fromString("f000aa01-0451-4000-b000-000000000000");
private static final UUID
UUID_CHARACTERISTIC_TEMPERATURE_CONFIG =
```

```
UUID.fromString("f000aa02-0451-4000-b000-000000000000");
```

Our results of service discovery, which we initiated in the last step would be delivered in the `onServicesDiscovered` method. Override the `onServicesDiscovered` method as a part of `BluetoothGattCallback` as shown next:

```
@Override
public void onServicesDiscovered(final BluetoothGatt gatt,
int status) {
  super.onServicesDiscovered(gatt, status);
  gatt.readCharacteristic(gatt.getService(UUID_IR_TEMPERATURE
  _SERVICE).getCharacteristic(UUID_CHARACTERISTIC_TEMPERATURE
  _DATA));
  }
```

Once the service discovery is finished, we instruct `BluetoothGatt` to read the Temperature Data characteristic through the code mentioned above.

12. As already pointed out, the Temperature Data characteristic supports Notifications and we can enable these notifications for periodic data updates for Temperature Data. Once we have successfully read the Temperature Data characteristic, we can enable Notifications for this characteristic as shown next while overriding the `onCharacteristicRead` method in the `BluetoothGattCallback` implementation:

```
@Override
public void onCharacteristicRead(BluetoothGatt gatt,
BluetoothGattCharacteristic characteristic, int status) {
  super.onCharacteristicRead(gatt, characteristic, status);
  if
(characteristic.getUuid().equals(UUID_CHARACTERISTIC_TEMPERATUR
E_DATA)) {
   //Enable local notifications
   gatt.setCharacteristicNotification(characteristic, true);
   //Enabled remote notifications
   BluetoothGattDescriptor desc =
characteristic.getDescriptor(CONFIG_DESCRIPTOR);
desc.setValue(BluetoothGattDescriptor.ENABLE_NOTIFICATION_VALUE
);
   gatt.writeDescriptor(desc);
  }
 }
```

Once the Notifications are enabled, whenever the Temperature Data is updated on the SensorTag, the app will receive the updated value in the `onCharacteristicChanged` method.

13. As already pointed out in the last step, we shall override the `onCharacteristicChanged` method so that we can receive the updated temperature value in order to parse and print it on the console for now:

```
@Override
public void onCharacteristicChanged(BluetoothGatt gatt,
BluetoothGattCharacteristic characteristic) {
 super.onCharacteristicChanged(gatt, characteristic);
 if
(characteristic.getUuid().equals(UUID_CHARACTERISTIC_TEMPERATUR
E_DATA)) {
   double ambient =
Utilities.extractAmbientTemperature(characteristic);
   System.out.println(ambient);
 }
}
```

The temperature data is in the following format:
`ObjectLSB:ObjectMSB:AmbientLSB:AmbientMSB,`. For extracting the data, we have created a separate class called `Utilities`. Add a separate class called `Utilities` to the project and introduce the following `extractAmbientTemperature` method in it:

```
public static double
extractAmbientTemperature(BluetoothGattCharacteristic c) {
        int offset = 2;
        return shortUnsignedAtOffset(c, offset) / 128.0;
}
```

The `extractAmbientTemperature` method makes use of the `shortSignedAtOffset` method, hence we would be adding that too to the `Utilities` class.

```
/**
 * Gyroscope, Magnetometer, Barometer, IR temperature
 * all store 16 bit two's complement values in the awkward
format
 * LSB MSB, which cannot be directly parsed as
getIntValue(FORMAT_SINT16, offset)
 * because the bytes are stored in the "wrong" direction.
 *
 * This function extracts these 16 bit two's complement
```

```
values.
 * */
private static Integer
shortSignedAtOffset(BluetoothGattCharacteristic c, int
offset) {
  Integer lowerByte = c.getIntValue(FORMAT_UINT8, offset);
  Integer upperByte =
c.getIntValue(BluetoothGattCharacteristic.FORMAT_SINT8,
offset + 1); // Note: interpret MSB as signed.
  return (upperByte << 8) + lowerByte;
}
```

The preceding code snippet has been sourced as is from `http://processors.wiki.ti.com/`.

We have enabled Notifications for the data characteristic and theoretically we should be able to sit back and just wait for the temperature sensor to read, update, and notify latest temperature values to us via the `onCharacteristicChanged` method. However, this is not the case, we are still missing a key step before we can get temperature updates successfully, which we will tackle in the next step.

14. If you were able to go over the documentation link, which we pointed out in step *11*, then there is a key detail mentioned in that document as shown next:

Figure 10: Details for temperature configuration characteristic

As per the preceding details, please note that by default, the temperature sensor is not enabled to record measurements. Hence, by default, our temperature sensor is in sleep mode; we need to bring it to active mode so that we can receive periodic notifications. We do so by overriding the `onDescriptorWrite` method in the `BluetoothGattCallback` implementation in the `MainActivity` class as shown next:

```
@Override
public void onDescriptorWrite(BluetoothGatt gatt,
BluetoothGattDescriptor descriptor, int status) {
    super.onDescriptorWrite(gatt, descriptor, status);
    enableConfigurationForCharacteristic(gatt,
descriptor.getCharacteristic());
}
```

As per the implementation of `onDescriptorWrite`, we will also need to implement the `enableConfigurationForCharacteristic` method in the `MainActivity` class as shown next:

```
private void
enableConfigurationForCharacteristic(BluetoothGatt gatt,
BluetoothGattCharacteristic characteristic) {
 if
(characteristic.getUuid().equals(UUID_CHARACTERISTIC_TEMPER
ATURE_DATA)) {
gatt.readCharacteristic(gatt.getService(UUID_IR_TEMPERATURE
_SERVICE).getCharacteristic(UUID_CHARACTERISTIC_TEMPERATURE
_CONFIG));
 }
}
```

And this is where the second important characteristic, the Configuration Characteristic, which we mentioned earlier, comes into play.

15. Following up from the last step, we shall read the Configuration Characteristic (and update it as a next step) so that we could eventually configure our temperature sensor to move from *sleeping* to *active* mode. For updating the configuration characteristic, update the pre implemented method `onCharacteristicRead` to the following:

```
@Override
public void onCharacteristicRead(BluetoothGatt gatt,
BluetoothGattCharacteristic characteristic, int status) {
 super.onCharacteristicRead(gatt, characteristic, status);
 if
(characteristic.getUuid().equals(UUID_CHARACTERISTIC_TEMPERATUR
E_DATA)) {
   //Enable local notifications
   gatt.setCharacteristicNotification(characteristic, true);
   //Enabled remote notifications
   BluetoothGattDescriptor desc =
characteristic.getDescriptor(CONFIG_DESCRIPTOR);
desc.setValue(BluetoothGattDescriptor.ENABLE_NOTIFICATION_VALUE
);
   gatt.writeDescriptor(desc);
 } else if
(characteristic.getUuid().equals(UUID_CHARACTERISTIC_TEMPERATUR
E_CONFIG)) {
   characteristic.setValue(new byte[] {0x01});
   gatt.writeCharacteristic(characteristic);
 }
}
```

After successful read, we write **0x01** to the Configuration Characteristic so that our Temperature Sensor is set to Active mode.

16. We are done with our implementation and now the `onCharacteristicChanged` method should be called for every temperature value update on the SensorTag. As a final step we can update the `onCharacteristicChanged` method to display live temperature updates to the user. Also, we can setup and include the data upload to Firebase backend so that our app can keep uploading periodic data updates to the remote server. We have setup Firebase numerous times now and would not be re-iterating it here. Our final code for UI updates and upload to backend is as follows:

```
@Override
public void onCharacteristicChanged(BluetoothGatt gatt,
BluetoothGattCharacteristic characteristic) {
 super.onCharacteristicChanged(gatt, characteristic);
 if
(characteristic.getUuid().equals(UUID_CHARACTERISTIC_TEMPERATUR
E_DATA)) {
   final double ambient =
Utilities.extractAmbientTemperature(characteristic);
   //Upload to Firebase Backend
   FirebaseDatabase database = FirebaseDatabase.getInstance();
   DatabaseReference myRef =
database.getReference("Temperature");
   myRef.setValue(ambient);
   //Update the UI
   runOnUiThread(new Runnable() {
    @Override
    public void run() {
     ((TextView)
findViewById(R.id.textView)).setText("Temperature: " + ambient
+ "\u00b0" + "C");
    }
   });
  }
}
```

If you run the app now and have an advertising SensorTag nearby, then you should see dynamic temperature updates coming in and the UI getting updated as shown in the following screenshot:

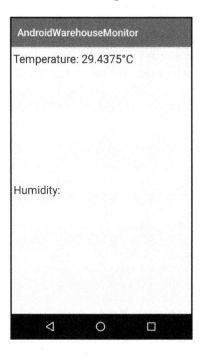

Figure 11: Dynamic temperature updates

Phew, that was something! And we are done with our Android implementation.

Note that if you run the app and are not able to see the devices getting discovered (in the logs or while debugging), then make sure that your phone has location switched on.

You should also be able to see the live updates on the Firebase backend, which matches the data being shown on the app:

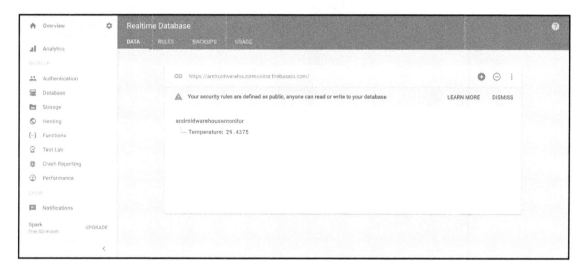

Figure 12: Dynamic updates to Firebase

We request you to go ahead and give a try to implement reading of Humidity Data yourself. If you find yourself struggling, the code we just implemented is available at the link mentioned next and it also has the implementation for reading Humidity Data.

Find the code for `AndroidWarehouseMonitor` at `https://github.com/madhurbhargava/AndroidWarehouseMonitor`.

As you would have noticed by now that our Apps are slowly adding more and more functionality as we progress through the chapters. Hence, for your convenience, we have broken down the functionality of the Android App that we just implemented and demonstrated the same in the following flowchart:

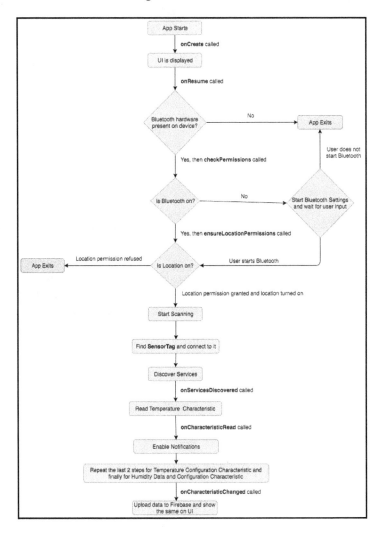

Figure 12.1 - Android Application Flow

Please use the above flowchart as your guidance tool while reviewing your Application Code implemented in this section. It will give you a bird's eye view of the code that we just implemented above.

Android being done, let's now move to iOS.

iOS

We covered reading the temperature data from the SensorTag in the Android sample. We take a slightly different approach this time and rather than implementing the same on iOS, instead, we cover the reading of Humidity Data. Without much ado, let's begin with the following steps:

1. We first start by creating a single view project in XCode by the name of `iOSWarehouseMonitor`. Similar to the previous chapters, Swift 3 would be the language of choice for this sample.

2. After project creation, create a very simple UI using the storyboard. Our UI will consist of a single humidity label to show the incoming humidity values as shown in the following screenshot:

Figure 13: iOS UI to display humidity values

3. We have already covered the initialization of CBCentralManager and scanning of devices using CBCentralManager; hence, we will not be repeating that here. If you find yourself struggling, then navigate to Chapter 3, *Building a Service Explorer App* and under iOS Sample code, go over steps 1 to 6.

4. Once we have added the code for scanning the peripherals, we need to filter out the SensorTag from the other broadcasting peripherals and then connect to it. For this, define a variable with the name for SensorTag in the ViewController class:

```
let NAME_SENSOR_TAG = "SensorTag"
```

Now, override the centralManager didDiscoverPeripheral function as we would be implementing our filtering and connection logic here as shown next:

```
public func centralManager(_ central: CBCentralManager,
didDiscover peripheral: CBPeripheral, advertisementData:
[String : Any], rssi RSSI: NSNumber) {
        let nameOfDeviceFound = (advertisementData as
NSDictionary).object(forKey:
CBAdvertisementDataLocalNameKey) as? String
        if let nameOfDeviceFound = nameOfDeviceFound {
            if
(nameOfDeviceFound.contains(NAME_SENSOR_TAG)) {
                print(peripheral.name!)
                self.centralManager.stopScan()
                // Set as the peripheral to use and
establish connection
                self.sensorTagPeripheral = peripheral
                self.sensorTagPeripheral.delegate = self
                self.centralManager.connect(peripheral,
options: nil)
            }
        }
    }
```

Note that you will also need to declare a CBPeripheral variable in the ViewController class as shown next:

```
var sensorTagPeripheral : CBPeripheral!
```

If you run the app now, then you should be able to successfully connect to a SensorTag if you have one broadcasting nearby.

5. If the connection was successful, then the `centralManager`
   `didConnectToPeripheral` method should be called via
   `CBCentralManagerDelegate` and that is where we need to initiate service
   discovery as shown next:

```
public func centralManager(_ central: CBCentralManager,
didConnect peripheral: CBPeripheral) {
        peripheral.delegate = self
        peripheral.discoverServices(nil)
    }
```

6. We are specifically interested in the Humidity Service and need to filter out the
   same from the list of services being discovered. For this, define the UUID for
   Humidity service in the `ViewController` class:

```
let HumidityServiceUUID = CBUUID(string: "F000AA20-0451-4000-
B000-000000000000")
```

The results of the service discovery can be explored in the `peripheral`
`didDiscoverServices` method, which is called by
`CBPeripheralDelegate` to deliver the results of the service discovery
request. Override `peripheral didDiscoverServices` in the
`ViewController` class as shown next:

```
public func peripheral(_ peripheral: CBPeripheral,
didDiscoverServices error: Error?) {
        if let services = peripheral.services {
            for service in services {
                if service.uuid == HumidityServiceUUID {
                    peripheral.discoverCharacteristics(nil,
for: service)
                }
            }
        }
    }
```

In the preceding code, we filter out the Humidity Service and place a
characteristic discovery request for the same.

7. Similar to temperature, as described in the Android sample, we are interested in `Data` and `Configuration` characteristics from the Humidity Service. Hence, we define them in the `ViewController` class:

```
let HumidityDataUUID = CBUUID(string: "F000AA21-0451-4000-
B000-000000000000")
let HumidityConfigUUID = CBUUID(string: "F000AA22-0451-4000-
B000-000000000000")
```

Also, our results for characteristics discovery will be delivered in the peripheral `didDiscoverCharacteristicsFor` service method, which is called by `CBPeripheralDelegate`. Override `peripheral didDiscoverCharacteristicsFor` service in the `ViewController` class as shown next:

```
public func peripheral(_ peripheral: CBPeripheral,
didDiscoverCharacteristicsFor service: CBService, error:
Error?) {
        // 0x01 data byte to enable sensor
        var enableValue = 1
        let enablyBytes = NSData(bytes: &enableValue,
length: MemoryLayout<UInt8>.size)
        // check the uuid of each characteristic to find
config and data characteristics
        for charateristic in service.characteristics! {
            let thisCharacteristic = charateristic as
CBCharacteristic
            // check for data characteristic
            if thisCharacteristic.uuid == HumidityDataUUID
{
                // Enable Sensor Notification
self.sensorTagPeripheral.setNotifyValue(true, for:
thisCharacteristic)
            }
            // check for config characteristic
            if thisCharacteristic.uuid ==
HumidityConfigUUID {
                // Enable Sensor
self.sensorTagPeripheral.writeValue(enablyBytes as Data,
for: thisCharacteristic, type:
CBCharacteristicWriteType.withResponse)
            }
        }
    }
```

In the preceding code, depending on the characteristic, we take the necessary action. If the characteristic discovered was Humidity Data characteristic, then we enable notifications on the same and if it is the Configuration characteristic, then we enable our Humidity Sensor from Sleep to Active mode in the exact similar manner like we did for the Temperature Sensor in the Android Sample.

8. Once the Sensor is active and the notifications are enabled, it should start broadcasting periodic data, which we can receive in the `peripheral didUpdateValueFor characteristic` method, which is called by `CBPeripheralDelegate` whenever new data is available. Override this method in the `ViewController` class:

```
func peripheral(_ peripheral: CBPeripheral, didUpdateValueFor
characteristic: CBCharacteristic, error: Error?) {
        if characteristic.uuid == HumidityDataUUID {
            let humidity = Utilities.getRelativeHumidity(value:
characteristic.value! as NSData)
            let humidityRound =
Double(round(1000*humidity)/1000)
            // Display on the humidity label
            labelHumidity.text = "Humidity:
"+String(humidityRound)
        }
    }
```

We parse the received data and update the same on the UI label.

9. The Humidity Data is structured as `TempLSB:TempMSB:HumidityLSB:HumidityMSB` and needs to be parsed before it can be presented to the user. For parsing this data, create a separate class called `Utilities` and define the `getRelativeHumidity` method in it:

```
class func getRelativeHumidity(value: NSData) -> Double {
        let dataFromSensor = dataToUnsignedBytes16(value:
value)
        let humidity = -6 + 125/65536 *
Double(dataFromSensor[1])
        return humidity
    }
```

The preceding method makes use of the `dataToUnsignedBytes16` method, which converts the characteristic's value to an array of 16-bit unsigned Integers, which can be implemented and added to the `Utilities` class as shown next:

```
class func dataToUnsignedBytes16(value : NSData) ->
[UInt16] {
        let count = value.length
        var array = [UInt16](repeating: 0, count: count)
        value.getBytes(&array, length:count *
MemoryLayout<UInt16>.size)
        return array
    }
```

This completes our implementation. If you run the app now and have a SensorTag broadcasting nearby, then you should see the humidity values updating dynamically on the screen as shown next:

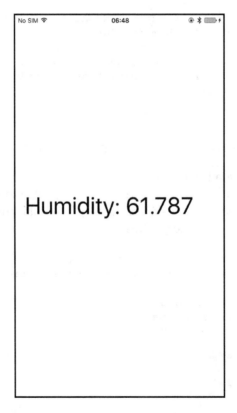

Figure 14: Dynamic humidity value updates

If you are able to see the humidity values getting updated dynamically on the screen as shown earlier, then congratulations! You have successfully read the Humidity Data from the SensorTag.

 Find the code for `iOSWarehouseMonitor` on the following link: `https://github.com/madhurbhargava/iOSWarehouseMonitor`.

This also marks the completion of both Android and iOS warehouse monitoring solutions. At this point our solution is ready to be presented to the board members for their approval.

The SensorTag offers you 10 Sensors and we have only explored 2. We encourage you to expand on the knowledge that we built in this chapter and explore other solutions around different Sensors.

Practical Applications

Apart from warehouse climate monitoring, we shall discuss other real-life use cases of temperature and humidity Bluetooth Low Energy data loggers to give you a better understanding of the domains, where similar solutions to the one we discussed earlier can be applied with minimal changes.

Idemitsu Museum of Arts

Idemitsu Museum of Arts in Tokyo uses Bluetooth Low Energy temperature and Humidity Data loggers to manage the indoor climate in the museum from preserving antique pieces of art, in a similar fashion as depicted in the following figure:

Figure 15: Wireless climate monitoring in museums; source: `www.onsetcomp.com`

This museum stores Japanese artefacts such as Japanese paintings, calligraphy, and pottery for public exhibitions.

 For a full case study, visit `http://www.onsetcomp.com/content/ bluetooth-data-loggers-streamline-museum-environmental- monitoring`.

These artefacts, specifically paintings, are rare antiques, drawn in the 16th Century in Japan. Preservation of these antiques is of vital importance since they represent the cultural heritage of Japan. Most of these paintings are drawn on paper and it is vital that the indoor climate of the museum, specifically temperature and humidity, are closely monitored as unmanaged climatic conditions can harm these delicate paintings.

Salisbury Cathedral

Salisbury Cathedral is home to *Magna Carta*, a document of historical importance, which is around 800 years old.

 You can find the full case study at `http://www.onsetcomp.com/learning/ application_stories/bluetooth-temperature-logger-protects-magna- carta`.

This best surviving copy is preserved in a completely sealed glass case equipped with Bluetooth Low Energy temperature and Humidity Data loggers so as to prevent deterioration of the document due to weather parameters.

Summary

If you arrive here after completing all the code samples, then give yourself a solid pat on the back, since we covered a really wide ground in this chapter by implementing a detailed and commercially viable IoT solution built over Bluetooth Low Energy. This chapter was significantly a notch up from the others considering the complexity involved and we do hope that after completing it you already feel promoted to the next level with all the knowledge we gained in this chapter.

We are very curious to know that what you will build next with all this new knowledge at hand. Feel free to drop us a line in case you come up with a cool solution revolving around BLE, Sensors, and IoT.

With this, we now move on to the next chapter, which attempts to explore the future of Bluetooth Low Energy and eventually IoT.

7
Going Further

"I'm still learning"

- Michelangelo (at the age of 87)

This chapter will be the conclusion of the journey which we started six chapters back. We will be covering the following topics in this chapter to enhance your knowledge about Bluetooth 5, which is the latest release by the **Bluetooth Special Interest Group (SIG)**:

- Bluetooth 5
- Practical Use Cases
- Future of BLE
- Future of IoT

Moving further in this chapter, we will be introducing various practical use cases of IoT built using Bluetooth Low Energy, which are already being used by people in their day-to-day lives. These cases will give you a bird's-eye view of Bluetooth Low Energy applications with respect to IoT in different domains.

Eventually, we will discuss what the future holds for BLE and IoT, and we shall conclude by consolidating what we have learned so far.

Bluetooth 5

Bluetooth 5 was announced by the Bluetooth SIG on June 16, 2016 to be arriving in late 2016, and it was finally officially unveiled on December 7, 2016. As per the initial advertisement, it was announced to have *"Quadruple the range of its predecessor, double the speed, and 8 times the broadcasting capacity,"* for low energy connections.

Let's examine each of the factors one by one so that we can understand the practical implications of each of them.

8 Times the Broadcasting Capacity

Currently, Bluetooth Low Energy (4.2) offers advertising packet sizes of 31 bytes and BLE 5 allows this to increase by a factor of eight, that is, the broadcasting capacity of a BLE 5 device would be 255 bytes.

To understand this better, let's perform a small experiment. In Chapter 5, *Beacons with Raspberry Pi*, we configured our Raspberry Pi to broadcast a URL as an Eddystone Beacon. We shall repeat the same experiment here, however, with a little twist.

In terms of the setup, this time, instead of the Raspberry Pi, we shall be configuring a MacBook Pro to broadcast the EddyStone Beacon.

 Please note that for this experiment, instead of the MacBook Pro, you can still configure a Raspberry Pi as shown in Chapter 5, *Beacons with Raspberry Pi*, or simply use an App like *Beacon Toy* on an Android Mobile device to act as the Eddystone Beacon. We are just using a MacBook so that we can introduce you to the various ways of creating an EddyStone Beacon.

The prerequisites for the experiment are a Mac/MacBook running OSX 10.10 or later (with Bluetooth 4 capable hardware), Xcode, and the latest Node.js. To be exact, our own setup for the following experiment consists of a MacBook Pro running on macOS Sierra version 10.12.6, with Xcode version 8.3.2, and Node version 8.0.0.

1. Please create a new directory in the Downloads directory. Give it a name of your choice (preferably without spaces). Open the terminal, navigate to the newly created directory, and execute the following commands:

```
$ npm install --save eddystone-beacon
$ node -e "require('eddystone-
beacon').advertiseUrl('https://bluetooth.com');"
```

2. If you have an Android smartphone, then you can download and install the Physical Web app from the Play Store (for iOS/iPhone users, you can download the Physical Web Browser App by BKON Connect or something similar from App Store) and if you launch the app, then you should see the Beacon broadcasting the URL, as shown next:

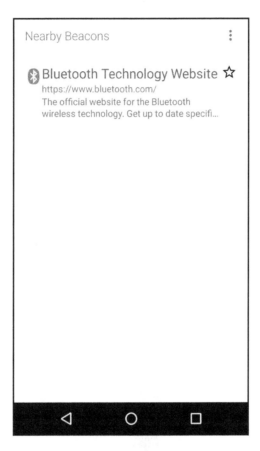

Figure 1: Received Eddystone URL broadcast

3. Now, here comes the twist. In the terminal, stop the Beacon broadcast by pressing *Ctrl + C*. Now update the URL as shown in the following command and execute the command again:

```
$ node -e "require('eddystone-
beacon').advertiseUrl('https://developer.android.com');"
```

As soon as you run the command, you should see an error, as shown next:

```
                   :NodeBeaconBroadcast                    $ node -e "require('eddystone-beacon').advertiseUrl('https://developer.android.com');"
/Users/                    /Documents/NodeBeaconBroadcast/node_modules/eddystone-url-encoding/lib/encode.js:16
    throw new Error([
    ^

Error: Encoded URL (https://developer.android.com) is too long (max 18 bytes): 19 bytes
```

Figure 2: Beacon broadcast error

Can you guess what happened? Well, what happened is this: the MacBook Pro that we are using to run this test is running on Bluetooth version 4.2, which you can confirm by navigating to **System Report** as shown here:

1. Click on the **Apple** menu.
2. Select **About this Mac**.
3. Click on the **System Report...** button in the dialog that comes up.
4. Select **Bluetooth** from the left sidebar underneath **Hardware**.
5. Scroll down the list on the right until you come across **LMP Version**, as shown next:

Hardware	MacBook Pro	
▼ Hardware	Bluetooth Power:	On
ATA	Discoverable:	Off
Audio	Connectable:	No
Bluetooth	Auto Seek Pointing:	On
Camera	Remote wake:	On
Card Reader	Vendor ID:	0x05AC
Diagnostics	Product ID:	0x8290
Disc Burning	HCI Version:	4.2 (0x8)
Ethernet Cards	HCI Revision:	0x12B7
Fibre Channel	LMP Version:	4.2 (0x8)
	LMP Subversion:	0x2192
	Device Type (Major):	Computer

Figure 3: Bluetooth settings on a Mac

And there is the root cause of the problem. As you can see, the experiment is being run on hardware that supports Bluetooth 4.2, hence the advertising packet just has a size of 31 bytes. From these 31 bytes, only 18 bytes are available for the user payload (for more details on the actual advertising packet payload, refer to the *Creating a beacon with Raspberry Pi* section in Chapter 5, *Beacons with Raspberry Pi*) and as soon as our URL data exceeds 18 bytes, the Beacon cannot be broadcasted.

Bluetooth 5 resolves this problem for us by increasing the advertising packet size from 31 bytes to 255 bytes, which will enable us to pack much more data in the advertising packet and broadcast it. Specifically for Eddystone-URL Beacons, it means that we would be able to broadcast much more complex URLs without using a URL shortening service.

Doubles the Speed

Bluetooth 5 promises to double the **Connection speed**, **Network data rate**, and **Data throughput** as outlined in the following table:

	BLE 4.2	BLE 5	BLE 5 Long Range (S=2)	BLE 5 Long Range (S=8)
Connection speed	1 Mbps	2 Mbps	1 Mbps	1 Mbps
Network data rate	1 Mbps	2 Mbps	500 Kbps	125 Kbps
Data throughput	800 Kbps	1400 Kbps	380 Kbps	109 Kbps
Error Correction	None	None	FEC	FEC
Bluetooth 5 Requirement	Mandatory	Optional	Optional	Optional

Figure 4: BLE 4.2 versus BLE 5, speed and throughput comparison; source: www.androidauthority.com

For consumers, this means that they would now be able to sync their Bluetooth 5 devices much faster compared to the Bluetooth 4.2 devices. For example, a fitness tracker with a week's data which used to take 10 seconds (approximately) to sync, will, with Bluetooth 5, be able to sync in only 5 seconds.

Quadruples the Range

Apart from the double speed, Bluetooth 5 also promises to quadruple the range of broadcast. It promises a maximum speed of 48 Mbps for distances up to 300 meters. See a detailed speed distance comparison table between Bluetooth **Version 4.1**, **Version 4.2** and **Version 5**:

	Speed	Distance	Released Date	Bands	Backward Compatibility	New Hardware Requirement
Version 4.1	24MBs	100 m or 300 feet	4/12/2013	2.4 to 2.485 GHz	Yes	No
Version 4.2	24MBs	100 m or 300 feet	2/12/2014	2.4 to 2.485 GHz	Yes	For some feature
Version 5	48MBs	300 m or 985 feet	16/06/2016	2.4 to 2.485 GHz	No	Yes

Figure 5: BLE 4.1, BLE 4.2, and BLE 5, speed and distance comparison; source: iTechTics.com

Bluetooth 5 also introduces a new mode of operation known as long range mode. Devices operating in long range mode can sacrifice data rate to achieve longer range/distance of operation. Engineers at Texas Instruments have successfully tested the long range mode by connecting to a Bluetooth device 1.6 km away (yes, you read that right) with data throughput of 125 kbps. See the details of their exciting experiment at the link mentioned next.

 Navigate to the following link to see the experiment conducted by the engineers from Texas Instruments Inc, regarding Bluetooth 5 Long Range Mode: https://training.ti.com/long-range-cc2640r2f.

This means, with the new wave of Bluetooth 5 fitness trackers hitting the market, you could now leave your phone in the car for your future runs at the park rather than having it strapped to your arm.

The quadrupled range makes BLE 5 an interesting choice for the Internet of Things since devices can be connected over greater distances and cover larger surface areas (warehouses, malls, and so on).

Practical Use Cases

We have already seen BLE plus IoT use cases around Beacons and fitness trackers. In the following section, we cover some more practical usages/use cases of Bluetooth Low Energy-based IoT solutions, which are being deployed across various domains.

Philips Sonicare Toothbrush

The use case of Philips Sonicare Toothbrush presents a scenario where Bluetooth Low Energy together with IoT is helping to improve the oral health of individuals. Philips is a well-known Dutch company, which has primary divisions focused in the areas of electronics, healthcare, and lighting. Sonicare is the brand name of an electronic toothbrush produced by Philips.

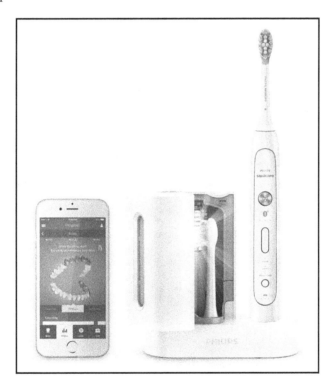

Figure 6: Philips Sonicare Toothbrush; source: `image.philips.com`

As shown in the preceding image, the Philips Sonicare toothbrush has a thick handle which contains the following sensors:

- Motion detector gyroscope
- Accelerometer
- Pressure sensor
- Scrubbing detector

Bundled with the toothbrush is an app, available on both Android and iOS platforms.

 To know more about Philips Sonicare toothbrush, visit `http://www.usa.philips.com/c-m-pe/electric-toothbrushes`.

The data from the previously mentioned sensors is collected in the toothbrush and can be synced to the app via Bluetooth Low Energy. This data, when processed, can be used to inform the user about his/her oral healthcare regarding items such as which areas in the mouth need more brushing and how much pressure should be applied while brushing. The data generated is synced and stored in a backend, and the reports generated can also be shared confidentially with the user's dentist.

Wahoo Balance Smartphone Scale

The Wahoo Balance Smartphone Scale keeps track of your weight and BMI by uploading your stats automatically via Wi-Fi:

Figure 7: Wahoo Smart Fitness Scale; source: www.thesimplemoms.com

Bundled with the scale is an app, which can connect to the weight scale over Bluetooth Low Energy and keeps a track record of weight, BMI, and body fat percentage over a period of time and can help the user visualize the same information.

 To know more about the Wahoo Fitness Scale, visit http://eu. wahoofitness.com/devices/accessories/wahoo-balance-smartphone- scale.

If you want to share your weight with others, such as a coach or a caregiver, the scale can upload your data automatically to registered accounts at MyFitnessPal.

iLumi Smart Bulb

The iLumi Smart Bulb presents a unique BLE plus IoT case study about home lighting and automation. iLumi is a Bluetooth Low Energy-controlled smart bulb, shown next:

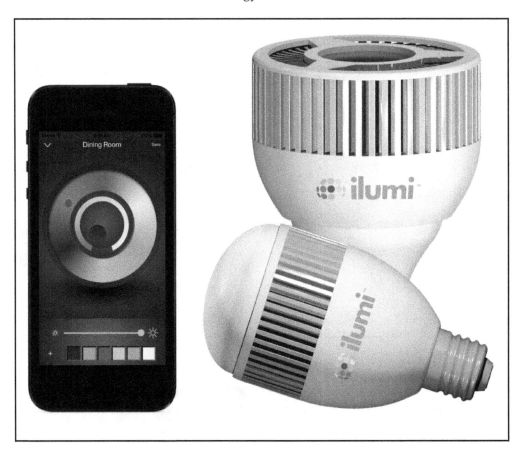

Figure 8: iLumi Smart Bulb; source: www.gadgetfreak.gr

iLumi's USP lies in its different way of working from other similar solutions available in the market, most of which require networking equipment and bridges.

 For more details about iLumi, visit https://ilumi.co/.

iLumi on the other hand can fit into any regular bulb socket and its color and dimming can be simply controlled by your smartphone via an app over Bluetooth Low Energy.

Eve Smart Light Switch

In the previous case study, we introduced the iLumi Smart Bulb, but what if you do not want to change the bulbs in your house yet still want to enjoy the benefits of an intelligent lighting system? In comes the Eve Smart Light Switch by Elgato:

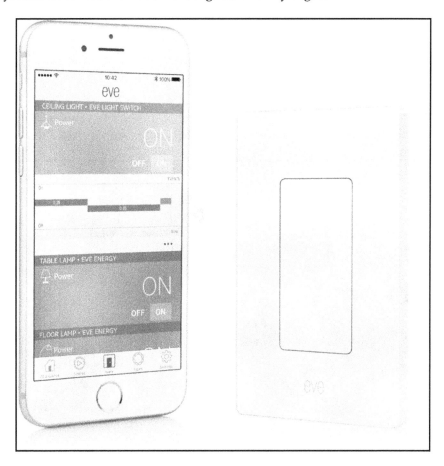

Figure 9: Eve Smart Light Switch and App; source: www.elgato.com

The Eve Smart Light Switch lets you keep the Bulbs and Lighting in your house intact and still lets you enjoy all the benefits of a smart home.

 To understand more about the Eve Smart Light Switch's capabilities, watch the video available at `https://www.youtube.com/watch?v=sQfc4bjqM6I`.

Fully compatible with Apple's home kit, this Light Switch can replace any of the existing light switches in the house. Once installed, you can simply pair it with your smartphone using the Elgato Eve app (available from the App Store), which can control the Switch via Bluetooth Low Energy. As well as controlling the switch via Bluetooth Low Energy, it also works just fine as a normal light switch.

Danalock

Danalock is an automated smart home locking solution by a company with the same name:

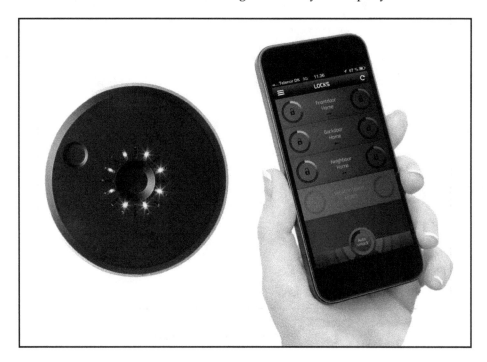

Figure 10: Danalock and corresponding smartphone app; source: `www.businesswire.com`

You can lock the Danalock via the smartphone app by sending data, which is AES-256 encrypted, over Bluetooth Low Energy.

 To know more about Danalock, visit `https://danalock.com/`.

It automatically detects via Bluetooth Low Energy whenever you are nearby and unlocks itself. Since the lock also has Wi-Fi capabilities, like any other IoT device, it can make its current state data available over Wi-Fi and you can check the state of the lock when you are away, over the internet.

Fobo

Fobo is a **tire pressure monitoring system (TPMS)** and we are mentioning it in this case study to point out how Bluetooth Low Energy is playing a role in the automobile industry:

Figure 11: Fobo TPMS; source: `www.fobobikesales.com`

Fobo is one of a kind, a Bluetooth Low Energy enabled, tire pressure monitoring system available for cars, motorbikes, and even bicycles. The installation is pretty simple; you just need to screw the sensor on the valve stem of the tire, as shown in the following image:

Figure 12: Installing Fobo sensors; source: www.my-fobo.com

Once you have screwed the sensor on to the tire of the automobile, you can now use the freely available Fobo smartphone app, create an account and activate the Sensor. On activation, almost immediately you can see the tire pressure and temperature in each of the tires via the sensors, as shown in the previous image.

 To know more about Fobo TPMS, visit https://my-fobo.com/.

Like many other BLE plus IoT devices, Fobo also has a cloud backend and allows user account creation and storage of a single sensor mapping to a single user's account. This also acts as a theft deterrent, since a stolen sensor cannot be used with a different tire and a different user account.

Tile

Tile is a small square-shaped piece of hardware that you can attach to your valuables (wallet, keys, smartphone, car, and so on) to mitigate the risk of losing them:

Figure 13: Tile and corresponding smartphone app; source: www.mobilefun.co.uk

A Tile can be attached to an item that the user has a risk of losing, and in case the user loses that item then he/she can locate it with the help of the Tile smartphone app.

The Tile smartphone app uses Bluetooth Low Energy to locate lost Tiles up to a 150-foot range. Tiles have in-built buzzers, which beep audibly so that the user can locate the source of sound and hence the item.

Each user's Tiles are mapped to his/her account. Tile also supports something known as *Community Find*. Community Find is a facility that can help you locate an item beyond the traditional 150-foot BLE range limit. The way Community Find works is as follows: when the Tile app runs, it is just not looking for your Tile, it is keeping a track of *everyone's* Tile (no matter whether it belongs to you or not). However, the user of the Tile app is deliberately kept oblivious to this fact due to reasons related to individual privacy. If any user loses his/her Tile beyond the 150-foot radius and needs to find it, then he/she can activate the *Notify When Found* feature in the Tile app. Now, if the lost Tile comes within the range of another user's Tile app, then the nearby user's application will send an anonymous update of that item's location to the item's owner.

To know more about Tile, visit `https://www.thetileapp.com/`.

Tile makes an excellent case study since it demonstrates how Bluetooth Low Energy is making its way into the consumer utility items domain.

HAPIfork

HAPIfork is a smart fork created by HAPI labs:

Figure 14: HAPIfork; source: `images.techhive.com`

Obesity is directly correlated to eating faster.

> For more information about the co-relation between excess weight and eating faster, visit `https://www.ncbi.nlm.nih.gov/pubmed/26100137`.

How many times have we heard our elders telling us the adage, "Eat Slowly!". However, it was always difficult to pinpoint exactly how slow was "slowly?" This is the problem that HAPIfork intends to solve for its users. The main goal of HAPIfork is to help its users eat slowly. If the user is eating too fast, then the fork vibrates gently with a visual cue of a red light indicator. If the user is maintaining a constant healthy pace, then the visual indicator stays green. HAPIfork comes bundled with a smartphone app for both Android and iOS, which can help you track your meals based on the following three important parameters:

- Meal duration
- Number of fork servings
- Time interval between two fork servings

The fork and the app communicate over Bluetooth Low Energy. The HAPIfork app also logs the meal data to the backend, which can help the user visualize and gather interesting insights about their meal data.

> To know more about HAPIfork, visit `https://www.hapi.com/product/hapifork`.

HAPIfork is an interesting case study since it demonstrates the usage of IoT plus Bluetooth Low Energy in the user's day-to-day activities.

Future of BLE

We have already outlined the various features of Bluetooth Low Energy 5 in the previous section, which add a significant improvement over Bluetooth Low Energy 4.2, especially in terms of range and speed. With these new improvements and promises, we will be seeing Bluetooth Low Energy penetrating more and more into our daily lives.

In this section, we will discuss a few of the products and technologies, based on Bluetooth Low Energy, that are under active development and expected to arrive in the consumer market soon.

Dreem

Dreem is a sleep solution by a company called Rhythm. Dreem intends to help users to sleep better:

Figure 15: Dreem by Rhythm; source: www.dreem.com

At its very core, Dreem is a wearable headband, which the user can wear while sleeping. The headband monitors and analyses users' sleep cycles.

 To know more about Dreem, visit https://dreem.com/.

However, note that monitoring sleep is not the USP of this product, since sleep monitoring has already existed for a long time. For example, Fitbit already provides sleep monitoring and presents users with insights about their sleep cycles and patterns through the Fitbit smartphone app in the form of graphs, as shown next:

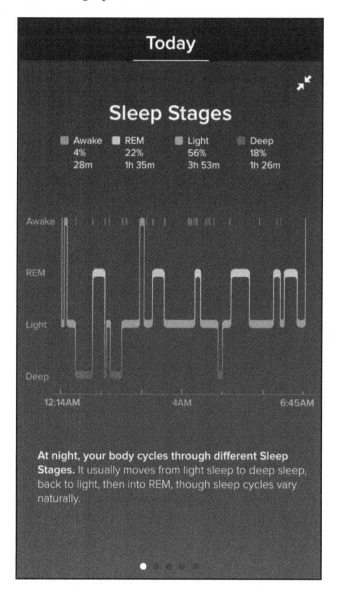

Figure 16: Fitbit sleep stages graph; source: blog.fitbit.com

The main USP of Dreem compared to other sleep monitoring solutions is that, apart from sleep monitoring and analysis, it can also provide sleep therapy to enhance the user's sleep and improve what is known as the user's overall sleep score. Bundled with Dreem is a smartphone app. The app and the headband communicate over Bluetooth Low Energy. The app can process and display the data recorded by the headband and keep the user informed about his/her sleep score:

Figure 17: Sleep score as shown in the Dreem smartphone app; source: itunes.apple.com

As of the time of writing this book, Dreem is only available for pre-order and not freely available in the consumer market.

BabyGigl

BabyGigl is a smart baby bottle holder, by a company known as *Slow Control* that monitors the milk fed to the baby via the bottle:

Figure 18: BabyGigl and corresponding app; source: www.slowcontrol.com

Additionally, it also keeps track of environmental data during meals.

　To know more about BabyGigl, visit http://www.slowcontrol.com/en/ baby-gigl/.

BabyGigl comes bundled with a smartphone app, which can communicate with BabyGigl over Bluetooth Low Energy. The app can also notify the parents regarding meal information about the meal provided by the caregiver to the infant. It also helps keep track of the baby's meals per day, per week, and per month.

As of the time of writing this book, BabyGigl is still under development and is not available in the market.

Future of IoT

Throughout this book, we have been discussing IoT in the light of Bluetooth Low Energy. In this section, we shall take a break from that and introduce other important technologies that IoT relies on apart from Bluetooth Low Energy. Eventually, we shall see some practical examples/applications/products that do not use Bluetooth Low Energy but play a major role in the IoT revolution.

Other Technologies

Although Bluetooth Low Energy is the cornerstone of IoT, it is, however,not the only cornerstone. Apart from Bluetooth Low Energy, IoT implementations as involve several other technologies which are worth mentioning:

1. **Zigbee**: Zigbee is a suite of communication protocols which are ideal for creating small personal area networks with low power digital radios, achieving transmission distances of 10-100 meters via line of sight communication. Zigbee has a defined data rate of 250 Kbps. These specifications make it ideal for home automation and low bandwidth needs. One of the popular use cases of Zigbee is the Philips Hue:

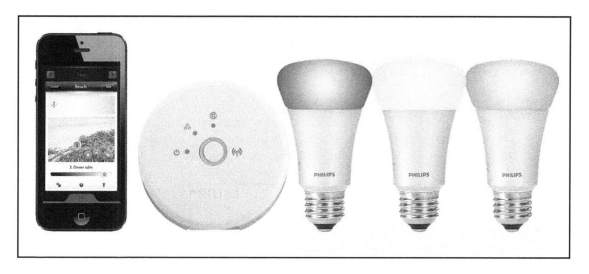

Figure 19: Philips Hue; source: image.philips.com

This is personalized smart wireless lighting (something similar to iLumi Smart Bulbs, which were introduced earlier; however, Philips Hue operates on Zigbee rather than BLE) operating in the following manner:

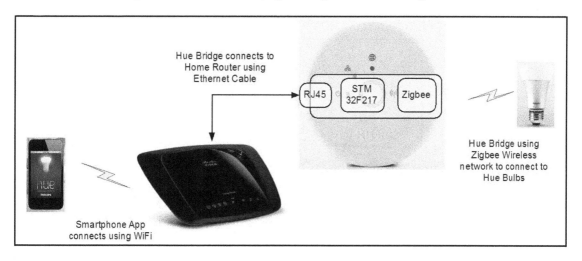

Figure 20: Workings of Philips Hue; source: images.anandtech.com

Bundled with the Hue smartphone app, as part of Hue Setup, the app connects to Wi-Fi and can send commands to a *Philips Hue Bridge* connected to the same network. This bridge can then translate these commands over Zigbee to the individual Philips Hue bulbs to change their color and light intensity.

2. **Bluetooth Mesh**: Mesh is a networking topology which allows establishing many-to-many device connections/communications. Currently, a Bluetooth device can support four to eight concurrent connections:

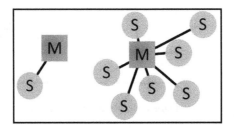

Figure 21: Bluetooth network piconet; source: www.sparkfun.com

As IoT capabilities grow, we will need to control dozens of devices via a single connection and Bluetooth Mesh can help us in doing just that:

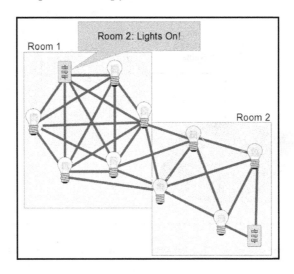

Figure 22: Mesh topology; source: blog.bluetooth.com

Bluetooth 5 will be a key turning point in Bluetooth Mesh networking due to its offering of quadrupled range.

Products

Apart from the technologies we have already mentioned, this discussion would not be complete if we fail to mention IoT products such as Amazon Echo and Google Home, which are ground-breaking IoT products of our times. These products are actually a glimpse into what the future holds for IoT:

Figure 23: Amazon Echo; source: www.sears.com

Amazon Echo is a smart speaker developed by Amazon, which is capable of understanding and translating voice commands into actionable events. Amazon Echo requires a wireless internet connection to work, and you can command Alexa, which is the voice assistant bundled with Amazon Echo. Using Alexa, you can request to play your favorite music from your Amazon account. Also, Amazon Echo can do several other things such as responding to questions about Google Calendar, checking the weather for you, and accessing Wikipedia articles.

 To see the capabilities of Amazon Echo in action, please watch this: `https://www.youtube.com/watch?v=FQn6aFQwBQU`.

Amazon Echo integrates with several third-party interfaces, including the Philips Hue. Using Amazon Echo, you can control the Philips Hue lights in your house via voice commands.

It rarely happens in the consumer market that a product lacks a competitor. For Amazon Echo, that role is played by **Google Home**:

Similar to Amazon Echo in many aspects, Google Home is a Smart Speaker by Google. You can give voice commands to Google Assistant, which is Alexa's counterpart. Comparatively, both products have their own strengths and weaknesses. For example, Google Home integrates better with the internet and is better at fetching information from the web, such as YouTube videos, and streaming them on the connected home television. However, Echo outperforms Home for shopping-related queries, which is Amazon's forte. Google Home brings in better sound quality and Amazon Echo provides a deep and wide integration with more (since Echo was introduced way earlier in 2014, compared to Home, which was Smart Home brands in 2016). Echo commands stronger Wi-Fi connectivity (hence a larger range of operation) and Home offers superior multi-user functionality. Google Home can also recognize and differentiate up to six different voices. Amazon Echo is more expensive than Google Home; however, Amazon has launched a cheaper version called Amazon Dot, albeit with lower sound quality.

Summary

If you consider why computers exist at all, it is to translate our human experience in the physical world to a virtual experience in the digital one. If computer vision algorithms are akin to making a computer "see," then BLE provides a way to both speak and feel between devices. Look around you at the inanimate objects in your home. Let your imagination run wild. "What would that object say to me if it could speak?" A houseplant might tell you its soil is dry. The dog food bowl might tell you it's empty. As the author of this book, I hope I've done my part to get you started and show you some possibilities. The rest is up to you.

This brings us to the conclusion of the final chapter of this book. We started this journey with a formal introduction to Bluetooth Low Energy in the light of IoT, continuing by designing BLE plus IoT apps for various sensors, Beacons, and fitness trackers. In this chapter, we tried to introduce various practical applications and examples to make you aware of the impact that Bluetooth Low Energy has on the world of IoT. This chapter would have given you a fair idea of the tip of the iceberg, which we tried to touch via this book. There is a lot more to explore out there and we hope that by now you would have a solid footing in Bluetooth Low Energy, both in theoretical and practical aspects.

We are really excited and cannot wait to see you applying this knowledge to real-world scenarios and we wish you all the best for your future projects and endeavors. If you build something cool, do drop us a line.

Index